TRIBUTES

"My Brother, I applaud your lifetime of service to humanity in the great cause of world peace. I will always remember our meetings with much joy."

Nelson Mandela
President of South Africa and Nobel Peace Laureate

"I am so pleased with all the good work you are doing for world peace and for people in so many countries. May we continue to work together and to share together all for the Glory of God and for the good of man."

Mother Teresa
Nobel Peace Laureate

"Your loving heart and profound wisdom are a matter of my boundless admiration."

Mikhail Gorbachev
President of the USSR and Nobel Peace Laureate

"Sri Chinmoy enriched the lives of countless others and served as a model of generosity and discipline to those he met, fostering an atmosphere of compassion, harmony, and unity...His legacy of kindness, reflection, and resolve will endure for many years to come."

Bill Clinton
42nd President of the United States of America

" Following the Indian tradition, he is one who ever revitalizes. The mutual friendship that unites us is proof of the deep resonance that can exist between initiates devoted to the cause of spirituality on earth."

"... it is a very rare thing to find a genuine representative of spirituality nowadays. This is what we feel in the presence of Sri Chinmoy – authenticity."

Pir Vilayat Khan
Head of the Sufi Order in the West

"Sri Chinmoy was a great man. God is smiling to know the immense good he has accomplished and encouraged in others. In a world of suspicion, hostility and conflict, he worked tirelessly to bring the different faiths together and inspired many to emulate."

Archbishop Desmond Tutu
Nobel Peace Laureate

"You have dedicated your life to the service of humanity and have brought together millions of people worldwide in the spirit of friendship and oneness."

Girija Koirala
Prime Minister of Nepal four times

"Your remarkable accomplishments have helped to ensure a better world for humankind."

Jean Chrétien
Prime Minister of Canada

"I regard Sri Chinmoy's work as one of the real treasures of the 20th and 21st centuries, probably the most powerful pillar of a culture of peace that currently exists."

Vladimir Petrovsky
Under-Secretary-General of the United Nations

"Sri Chinmoy is a miraculous model of the abundance in the creative life, and I can only hope that I may someday participate in that cosmic fountain of stillness and profound energy which he inhabits."

Leonard Bernstein
Composer and conductor

"Your consciousness knows no frontiers, your compassion knows no bounds and your horizons are as vast and limitless as those of the firmament itself...All India is proud of you."

Lakhan Mehrotra
Secretary to the Government, Ministry of External Affairs

AN
UNCONVENTIONAL PURSUIT

AN UNCONVENTIONAL PURSUIT

*One Woman's Spiritual Journey With
The Eastern Master Sri Chinmoy*

Kinkani Mursinna

*Heart Sky Unlimited
Pacifica, California*

Heart Sky Unlimited
P.O. Box 1651
Pacifica, California 94044 USA

Copyright © 2016 Kinkani Mursinna

All rights reserved.

No part of this book may be reproduced in any form or by any means, electronic or mechanical, including photography, recording, or by any information storage or retrieval system or technologies now known or later developed, without permission in writing from the publisher, except by a reviewer who may quote brief passages in a review.

Library of Congress Cataloging-in-Publication Data is available.

ISBN 978-0-9976283-0-2
First Printed Edition

Front cover and interior design by
Jason Gallagher & Nijan Shrestha

Back cover design by
Curve Nepal / Nijan Shrestha

Front cover and title page photos by
Bitapi Solomon

All other photos and aphorisms printed with permission by
the New York Sri Chinmoy Centre

Printed in Nepal

CONTENTS

PREFACE .... *xi*

Chapter One
THE VOID 3

Chapter Two
GIRL MEETS GURU 6

Chapter Three
THE EARLY YEARS 10

Chapter Four
EMBRACING THE WORLD 47

Chapter Five
THE FIRST PARTING 55

Chapter Six
ROUND TWO–BACK ON THE PATH 63

Chapter Seven
THE PEACE RUN 66

Chapter Eight
MY SPIRITUAL NAME 73

Chapter Nine
PRAYERS ANSWERED 75

Chapter Ten
OFF AGAIN 82

WANTING 87

About The Author 89

About Sri Chinmoy 91

FOREWORD

Lokendra Bahadur Chand
Chairman
and
Former Prime Minister of Nepal

लोकेन्द्र बहादुर चन्द
अध्यक्ष
राष्ट्रिय प्रजातन्त्र पार्टी
National Democratic Party

Central Office, Kathmandu, Nepal
Tel:01-6630427(R)

Message of Goodwill

In her childhood the author was blessed with a dream in which she came across Divine Light. For a few moments peace permeated her heart and she realized what actual peace, in a real sense, meant. Of course, it was a dream. She awoke and had to be absorbed in the day-to-day affairs of modern life.

In her life she had all the amenities and opportunities that a well-to-do family in the USA had. Her progress in material terms was also more than satisfactory. In spite of this she often felt that something very important was missing in her life. There was a void. Her worldly efforts as well as achievements were an exercise in futility. She felt that nothing would satisfy her unless the void in her was filled with something. But how and from what it could be done she did not know. That was the reason that she often fell into despair. She was exactly in that state of mind in which Arjuna, the foremost warrior of ancient India, had to undergo.

In the Indian subcontinent the Great War of Mahabharata had broken and for it warriors were waiting for the signal of Arjuna, who had to declare his readiness by blowing his conch shell. But in the midst of war Arjuna fell into despair. For him there was no purpose of fighting, killing and becoming victorious only to enjoy the luxuries of life for a very short span of time. Overwhelmed by melancholy he was about to run away from the battlefield. In that juncture Lord Krishna taught him about truth, soul and his Dharma (duty) that was, at that point of time, to participate in the war without caring for the outcome. The content of the *Gita*, the Jewel of Eastern philosophy, has been these teachings. There are 18 chapters in it and the first chapter describes the state of despair of Arjuna. Gradually, he comes out of it and performs his Dharma (duty). This first chapter is named, "Yoga of Dispondency (Vishad)." It is admitted that Dispondency is also yoga, which pushes and prods an individual to discover peace in the real sense of the term. So we can infer that the despair of the author was in a right place that made her restless to find out a way to give worth to her existence;

she embraced meditation. In her pursuit of peace she was lucky enough to meet Sri Chinmoy, an enlightened person, as Guru. Arjuna had Lord Krishna and she had Sri Chinmoy to dispel all confusions, anxieties and despondencies. Guru, like a lighthouse in a sea, made her journey easy and straight so she could fulfill her yearning.

An Unconventional Pursuit is an account of general human beings who are, in general, confused, sad and prone to be guided by their lower instincts. It is also an account of relentless struggle or devotion (Sadhana) of the same human being to attain a peaceful and happy life, as well as a life in which continuous Sadhana enables him to raise to a higher level of mind set and behavior.

The book appeals to different groups of mankind. It is useful for those too who have no interest in the inner world or spirituality, as it will fulfill their academic purpose. For those who believe in spirituality it is a real guide in the pursuit of peace and love and also in balancing the inner and outer self. I cannot help appreciating the author for her fine and useful work. I remember vividly those moments that I spent in the presence of Sri Chinmoy in Kathmandu. His personality was attractive and charming, and his busy schedule and punctuality impressed me. I could not put some of my queries to him about the problems confusing me because of his busy schedule. Had I done it, I am sure I would be leading a more happy and satisfied life.

Lastly, I participated in the unveiling ceremony of Sri Chinmoy's statue at Nagarkot near our capital, Kathmandu. I still cherish the memory of that soulful atmosphere and the peace that my heart realized there.

I wish happiness, forthcoming progress and grand success in the life of Kinkani Mursinna.

Thank you.

Lokendra Bahadur Chand
Chairman, National Democratic Party
and
Former Prime Minister of Nepal

PREFACE

A student of the spiritual Master, Sri Chinmoy, recounts her life-enriching experiences while practicing the teachings of an Eastern philosophy in a Western world. She highlights the pitfalls and struggles, as well as the profoundly moving moments of connectedness with a higher consciousness. It is written from the perspective of one who has left a spiritual path that once cradled her life, but that lives on in her heart and manifests in her life despite the separation. This book was written to offer inspiration to anyone seeking greater fulfillment in life, and to shed light on a genuine God-realized Master.

Sri Chinmoy read this book about six months before his passing and offered Kinkani his extreme gratitude for writing it.

A special thanks to

Adarini Inkei

for her photographs,

to

Palyati Fouse

for an undying

friendship

and to

Sri Chinmoy

for his inner guidance.

Sri Chinmoy visited Nepal in 1994 and 1999. In 1994, the mountain, Ghenge Liru, part of the Langtang mountain range, which stands in proximity to the statue was dedicated as a Sri Chinmoy Peace Mountain.

GRATITUDE TO NEPAL

I offer my deepest gratitude to Nepal and her people. It is here that I felt the quintessence of my Guru's teachings. In 2014, while trekking the Annapurnas to experience the majesty and divinity of the Himalayas, I also discovered the inherent spirituality of her people. From the guide and porter, Krishna Pokharel, who wholeheartedly embraced a difficult role with exuberance and joy, to the hotel Club Himalaya that so graciously hosts a life-size statue of my Guru, Sri Chinmoy. And to Nabraj Ghimire(RAJ), the owner of Good Karma Trekking, whose receptivity and enthusiasm towards this book was like no other. It is because of Raj that this story, so many years since it was written, is now available in hard copy.

Fifty percent of the book profits will be donated to the Good Karma Foundation, which Raj established after the earthquake of 2015. It provides educational materials and scholarships to the children of Nepal.

To anyone who visits Nepal and resonates with this story, I encourage you to visit Sri Chinmoy's statue at the Club Himalaya in Nagarkot. His living presence is in that statue. When I meditated there, at the feet of my Guru, it was exactly like he was there. I will forever hold that experience dear to my heart, as I will hold Nepal and the striking magnificence of her outer heights and inner depths.

Nepal, Nepal, Nepal, Nepal.
Within, without a self-offering heart.
Gurkha, to your indomitable strength,
Physical and spiritual, I bow.
Nepal, in you shines a oneness-heart
Of a Hindu and a Buddhist.
Indeed, this is a gift supreme
Of your consciousness-light
For the world at large.

- Sri Chinmoy

AN UNCONVENTIONAL PURSUIT

Chapter One

THE VOID

The door opened and, filled with the sense of wonder, I gazed into a huge, circular room of shimmering white. The white, so pure in essence, seemed more like opaque glass. It was as if light glinted off every molecule in the room, emblazing my eyes with a brilliance that almost distorted the figure sitting in the center.

On a throne-like chair sat a luminescent form. Its body of light was adorned in a white that appeared more solid than the room. Without hesitating I joyfully walked toward the faceless figure and curled up in his lap. I felt like a small child, safe and secure, in the lap of her Father. With a sense of surety I knew I had reached my goal.

Bathed in bliss, I awoke from a dream that would remain in my memory forever. I wrote about it in a journal I was required to keep for a creative writing class I took in college. Other than being struck by its vividness, it didn't mean much to me then. But it sure impressed my professor. He thought it was the most amazing dream he had ever read, and kept repeating that I must be a really evolved soul.

I definitely felt different from most teenagers, but his comments seemed a little over the top. He had a keen interest in Eastern philosophy and practiced meditation regularly. So to him my dream represented spiritual enlightenment. He never looked at me the same again.

In retrospect, that dream makes more sense. Perhaps it was a premonition of what lay ahead and a manifestation of my deepest yearning. A yearning that started as far back as I can remember.

> *We are nothing short of God's own Dream that is being unfolded for the Transformation of earth's ignorance-Life into heaven's perfection-light.*
>
> —Sri Chinmoy

I was born lucky, from an economic standpoint anyway. My parents were educated and had good paying jobs. And although they wanted the same for their children, my mother often reminded us that she didn't bring kids into the world just to survive. She wanted us to make the world a better place.

Perhaps because of her wish or perhaps because I never had to struggle just to survive, as so many kids in the world do, I continuously found myself pondering the "What's it all about?" question. Even as a very young girl I'd seek out secluded places in the nature that surrounded our home, just to be alone in silence. I'd listen to the wind through the leaves, or watch clouds sailing overhead. Practically anything in nature made me look inward and ponder; look inward and feel; look inward and long for peace or love or something I could hold onto and feel whole.

And so it went, year after year, until childhood was over and I hurdled into an adult. Fortunately, or unfortunately, all the same propensities followed me. While in college I still sought out nature's solace, even choosing to study in an open field overlooking the ocean, surrounded by redwoods, rather than some stuffy library. In fact, it was that very field on the campus of UC Santa Cruz where I had my most intense feeling of exasperation. I was eighteen.

It was like having my life flash before me; only it seemed to include everybody's life. I was seeing everything I had been given: a college education, a chance to follow any profession I wanted, my own car, a supportive family and friends, and the privilege to live in a beautiful country filled with opportunity. Then I saw the struggle of poverty that plagues so many others, the enormous effort that millions of people make throughout their lives just to achieve what I had simply been given.

I felt incredibly fortunate yet unbelievably empty. I thought to myself, "If what I have is what so many others long for and still I feel so unfulfilled then what is the point of striving for it?" And it's not that I didn't know the value of hard work applied to a goal. I had plenty of those experiences. Even so, I thought, if I were to achieve the profession of my choice and live in a beautiful home with a loving family, all the things we are raised to believe in as real success, clearly, my heart would still echo pangs of emptiness.

Without a doubt, I had entered the void. Surely there was more to life than outer achievements. And so it seems, from that very moment, atop that strikingly beautiful field, I sent forth my most fervent request: to find real fulfillment, to know its source and to understand its purpose. Perhaps my dream held the answer.

CHAPTER TWO
GIRL MEETS GURU

It was after I met my Guru, Sri Chinmoy, that I discovered what the emptiness was all about. Guru, as his students fondly called him, referred to my experience of the void as "divine discontent." Apparently, it was a good thing. I credit it with leading me to pursue the spiritual way of life. But it wasn't until I had learned to meditate that I came to the realization that true fulfillment involves spiritual aspiration, rather than worldly or material aspiration. Meditation allowed me to consciously connect with my heart's qualities, bring them forward and offer them in my daily life. It is no wonder that self-giving is such a powerful fulfiller. And lucky for us, the more a quality is manifested the greater it becomes.

I also gained a clearer understanding of what meditation really is: with our concentrated effort we invoke the Light of our soul: a spark of God, or more personally put, the Supreme. It permeates our entire being, awakening the sleeping giants of inner peace, power, love and oneness. The list of giants seems endless, but each awakens with even the slightest attention. That's probably why Guru would say that our ultimate realization would be 99% God's Grace and 1% personal effort. As his aphorism aptly puts:

There is only one thing to do,
And that thing is to conquer the noise
Of the outer life with the silence
Of the inner life.

Understanding the relationship between these two worlds: the inner and outer, and learning to balance them in a way that allows both to co-exist, be nurtured and develop without becoming fanatical in either direction, would take the next twenty years to discover. Truly, it is an art. Few perform this art more ardently and more gracefully than the Master, Sri Chinmoy, himself. It is one reason, I believe, we are given Masters from age to age. They are reminders, as well as teachers, of the balance we can all strive for as we slowly evolve into our own divinity. The key, it seems, is to focus on the inner life with the view of transforming the outer life.

I first discovered who Sri Chinmoy was, or any spiritual Master for that matter, when I returned to San Diego for the summer break of my sophomore year in college. I had transferred to UC Berkeley after I could no longer stand the pretentious hippies of Santa Cruz. Doing something because its cool or hip, rather than an expression of genuineness, has never sat well with me. At Berkeley, at least, people seemed more natural - how ironic. Now, many years later, I love visiting Santa Cruz. Except for the congestion all I see is beautiful surf, warm sun and majestic trees. Perhaps I've learned to overlook what I don't like.

While in San Diego a student of Sri Chinmoy was giving a free "Learn to Meditate" class. My brother and I decided to try it out. I would never have believed that something so simple could be so powerful until I tried meditation. Sitting quietly in nature as I had always done was clearly not meditation. It requires more than not talking or sensing your surroundings or your breath. Actually, it seems that meditation is not the absence of something, but the presence of something else: the longing for the divine. The instructor called this longing for divinity spiritual aspiration, and when it's coupled with our one-pointed concentration, meditation occurs.

As I sat in that chair listening to this man guide me through a focus exercise on my heart I thought I was entering heaven on earth. With 30 of us in a room of pin-drop silence, I felt, for the first time in my life, my spiritual heart center. It was like a warm, rotating disk, radiating light in every direction. The sense of peace was profound. That deep, abiding sense of satisfaction, so utterly fulfilling in its completeness, was mind-blowing. It felt as if my heart could burst and fill the universe at any moment. It was thrilling and exhilarating, yet so personal. Had I communed for that instant with my soul? Was this a gift from the Supreme, as if to show me the fruits of the spiritual life? What I do know is that experience, whenever I recall it, is as powerful and fresh as if it had just happened. Nothing in all my years to that moment could compare. That meditation was all I needed to fully understand its importance and necessity in my life.

I knew what I had to do, but it wasn't going to be easy. My mind revolted. It simply could not accept the idea of having a spiritual Master. My own inner experience while meditating was one thing, but becoming a student of a spiritual Master was going too far. There are standards to uphold: strict ones, and a lifestyle far different from society's norm.

Those unseen forces that seem to guide us must have known my mental struggles were too great and I soon found myself reading *Autobiography of a Yogi* by Paramahansa Yogananda. My brother had immediately become a student of Sri Chinmoy after attending a few more classes, while I debated the merits of having a teacher. I just couldn't let my ego down far enough to see their role.

Yogananda's book changed all that. It was like having a light turn on inside my head while asleep. All of a sudden: wham! I'm awake, gurgling, but awake.

I got it, admittedly, not without some apprehension, but I could see the purpose of having a spiritual guide.

So one year after that first eventful moment I became a student, or disciple, of Sri Chinmoy. He was now my Guru. I hadn't met him yet, but the inner relationship that was forming and would continue to form until today and on to tomorrow would change my perspective on almost everything.

CHAPTER THREE
THE EARLY YEARS

Meditating with a group was more powerful than I could have imagined. It is one of the standards all of Guru's disciples are required to uphold. There are several, and as time went on their importance became very clear. If it were not for the group meditation I would surely have never remained on a spiritual path. For it was that experience that helped me to develop the capacity to meditate alone.

Sri Chinmoy playing the esraj, one of a hundred different instruments he plays.

An Unconventional Pursuit

I'm the kind of person that always has to be doing something and usually at lightening speed. Since I loved sitting quietly in nature I thought meditating would come easy. I was so wrong. Sitting still and consciously practicing to quiet my mind was like pulling teeth. It became the most frustrating part of my day. As soon as I sat down to meditate all I could think of was everything I should be getting done. And if there was anything to clean, well, I could just as well forget about meditating.

Though we were only required to attend the Meditation Centre once a week, I regularly went twice. It was like entering another world. Entering that world actually started as I'd make my preparations to go. After a rejuvenating shower I'd carefully wrap my sari with its many evenly placed folds. Simply donning this Indian dress put me in a more spiritual frame of mind. One of the things Guru made very clear over the years was that everything has consciousness, and everything affects our consciousness in some way: either elevating it or lowering it. Clothes were no exception. He told us that the beauty, purity and modesty of the Indian sari would help to bring these qualities forward in the girls. The boys wore all white to help bring purity forward. Just the combination of boys in white and girls in saris was enough to elevate my consciousness. It looked so ethereal.

The 45-minute drive to the San Francisco Meditation Centre gave me another chance to shift gears. I took my Guru's advice and listened to his soulful music along the way. I really am lucky to have found such a talented Guru, one who is as prolific in writing as he is in music and art. It's never a problem finding something soulful to read, gaze at or listen to.

When I walked into the Meditation Centre I was immediately transported to a higher plane. Just sitting in that room, simply adorned with blue carpet, white walls and curtains, and a few of Guru's paintings, would make my mind peaceful. In front was a shrine, absolutely beautiful in its simplicity: a table covered in a white cloth with candles and flowers on each side of a very large picture of Sri Chinmoy meditating. But even more striking was the feeling in the room. There was a sense of peace so solid it could be cut with a knife. The peace seemed to compel us to stay quiet, dare we should disturb the tranquility. The consciousness of the Master filled that room. We all felt it. It made our Centre a truly sacred place.

Years later, I visited the meditation room of the San Francisco Zen Center and, there too, I felt the sublime peace that results from years of silent meditation. It makes me wonder how heavenly the world would feel if all humanity put forth a meditative vibration.

*You are aspiring.
That means you are lifting up
The consciousness of those who
Are around you.*

- Sri Chinmoy

I was still living in Berkeley, California when I first became a disciple. It was the beginning of my senior year at the University. And although classes were rigorous, I found myself, for the first time in my college career, sailing through school, effortlessly earning A's where previously B's and C's were the norm. Studying actually became an enjoyable pastime rather than an arduous chore.

I was absorbing knowledge like a parched plant after a desert rain. I had no doubt that my new discipleship, and all it contained, prompted this miraculous change. I was expanding my mind, learning to identify with the object of my concentration and increasing my receptivity to everything around me, including my studies. Previously, I had resisted my college commitment, reluctantly forcing myself to study. I was paddling upstream. Now, it was more like I had jumped onto a swiftly floating raft. As the years passed, however, I would find myself in a class five rapid. I was experiencing, first hand, the affects of the accelerated progress that is inherent in pursuing a spiritual path.

The first few months on the path were brimming with eye-opening experiences. I was beginning to see the tug-of-war that was constantly going on between my body, vital, mind, heart and soul: the five parts of the being often referred to by Sri Chinmoy.

Guru used the term "lower vital" to describe our negative emotions and sexual movements. Emotions like anger, lust, hatred, aggression, jealousy and depression have their source in the lower vital, while dynamism is housed in the "higher vital". In other words, our life energy can either take us closer to the Himalayan heights of consciousness or farther from it. Learning to recognize where our consciousness is focused is a major part of any spiritual seeker's life, and lies at the foundation of spiritual progress. Once recognized, it is the seeker's responsibility to consciously shift that focus to a higher place.

This is where having a Guru is so helpful. It's pretty easy to get stuck in some unprogressive state of being without knowing it, just look around you. The Guru, however, instantly sees it and can bring it to our attention. And lucky for me, there was the added benefit of having a plethora of ways to raise my consciousness. One of my favorites was singing Guru's songs. Soulful singing would immediately put me in my heart.

You can visualize these five parts of the being as rungs on a ladder, with the soul at the top. The soul is like our inner sun. It is all Light. Below the soul resides the heart. It is said that the heart houses the soul and is home to our positive emotions like gratitude, love and joy. It is the source of wisdom. These are the two highest parts of our being since they contain the most Light.

Below the heart, in terms of Light, rests the mind: incapable of oneness, always separating, analyzing and creating confusion. Then come the vital and the body. The body is steeped in lethargy. Left to its own it may never get out of bed. Luckily, the vital's dynamism enables the body to move. It's why daily exercise is important. That discipline is like the body's prayer; bringing Light into the physical through sheer movement. And if the exercise is done while focused on the heart, the physical body becomes inundated with Light. It's why Hatha Yoga can elevate our consciousness, as can any exercise done soulfully.

On Guru's path physical exercise is paramount. No part of the being is neglected; rather, our goal is to bring all parts of the being into harmony, which is why he calls his path the Path of Integral Yoga.

Over time, this concept became increasingly clear. It helped to discover the meaning of the word Yoga. Most of us equate it with a kind of slow-motion exercise called Hatha Yoga. But Yoga itself means union with God, and there are predominately three ways to reach that union.

One way is through service to others done without any need for recognition or compensation. We call it selfless service, or Karma Yoga. Another way is through knowledge gained by reading spiritual writings and practicing discrimination. It is called Jnana Yoga. Yet another is through devotion to God, called Bhakti Yoga. And since devotion cannot exist without the presence of love, the first step for Guru's disciples is to cultivate a love for the Divine.

On Sri Chinmoy's path all three of these Yogas are practiced, often daily. I was continuously impressed by the volume and variety of opportunities Guru created for us to integrate all these Yogas into our daily lives.

To fuel our knowledge we had over a thousand books to read from, in addition to thousands of songs. And, as if that wasn't enough, Guru would compose new aphorisms, poems and songs practically everyday.

For selfless service there seemed to be an endless supply of activities one could choose to assist with. I often spent months working in preparation for one of Guru's free concerts, and there were many. Really, the number of ways one could offer his or her services was only limited by our imagination.

Feeling a sense of devotion was equally important. It grew with the practice of meditation and continues to thrive as my appreciation for all things divine deepens.

Almost magically, through the Path of Integral Yoga, the five parts of the being evolve to work in harmony, increasing the heart's devotion, the mind's knowledge, the vital's dynamism, and the body's selfless work; and, little by little, we inch towards perfection.

A perfect existence, you could say, would be a being whose body, vital, mind, and heart listen to the dictates of the soul. It is, after all, the most illumined part of us. Our struggle then, as imperfect beings, is that we don't give charge to our higher parts. Instead, we follow our emotional whims, mental confusions and egos, and indulgent bodies. We treat the lower rungs like spoiled children: indulging them in every desire they express. We even go to the length of believing that our happiness will be the result, and justify our mind's decisions by believing it will bring satisfaction.

It is no wonder then, that so many human lives are spent fulfilling one desire after another. We're told it's a sign of success. We never learn who to listen to within us or how to tune in. So a Master comes and says, "Look, you're following the wrong leader. Your body, vital and mind will never guide you to your goal." But so few stop to listen. Why I chose to was pure grace. And for that grace I am eternally thankful.

Bringing Light into the physical is one of Guru's lessons that changed my life forever. Some of my most joyful and fulfilling experiences on the path involved this process, like the time Guru visited Santa Barbara. One evening he spontaneously asked us to run with him. We numbered about 75. The night air was still and the neighborhood silent as we soulfully jogged through the suburban streets of Santa Barbara, some still in saris. The thumping of feet, like the drumming of an ancient warrior tribe, echoed the trance-like vibrations that played in our hearts. We were meditating and running at the same time. It was the first of hundreds of lessons where I would learn the art of bringing a meditative consciousness into everyday activities. Meditation was not something to be achieved only by sitting still, but something to strive to accomplish while doing everything. Staying focused on the heart, bringing that Light forward and infusing it into every thought and action would become my lifelong goal. Having a Master who existed in that state at all times, even while scolding or joking with us, showed me it was possible.

What I came to experience was that Sri Chinmoy's level of consciousness was so vast and so high it was beyond my comprehension. There was no bearing in my perception that could grasp his consciousness. All I could do was either jump into it or let him jump into mine.

There have been many experiences of "jumping into the Master's consciousness", but one had tremendous intensity. I was being awarded a gift from Guru for being a part of a team that ran across America to spread the message of peace. During the moments of meditative silence, as I stood in front of my Master, his hand on one side of the gift and mine on the other, our eyes locked on one another, I felt every drop of my being flow into my Master's eyes. Eyes that were more like pools of light than human eyes. It was like stepping over the threshold of the earthly plane into an unknown world of sublime beauty and love. An exquisite peace, both soft and powerful, enveloped me. I wished, in that moment, that it would never end. I was swimming in a sea of effulgence that felt like perfection itself. I was like a baby in a womb: totally taken care of and embraced with no outer contact. I was inside my Master's consciousness, a drop floating amidst the ocean. There was a sense of completeness with nothing to be done.

When it ended I did everything I could to hold onto that experience. I wouldn't talk or even look at anybody else. I didn't even want to think, less a thought might disturb the perfection. Such moments between a Master and disciple are precious reminders of what lies ahead. It's like making a goal. You've scored. You've tasted the fruits of all your efforts, but only for an instant. Then you're back again, ball in hand, maneuvering and discerning, using all your skills and training to try to reach the goal again, and again, and again. How sweet it will be to reach that final goal, to become that goal once and for all.

Another benefit of physical exercise that most disciples experience is transcending one's previous capacities. Self-transcendence is another cornerstone of Guru's path. He would tell us that the Supreme is always transcending His own consciousness. God is not a static entity; therefore, we should aspire to continuously transcend our own consciousness. And since any accomplishment on one level helps us on all other levels, transcending physical achievements was an easy start.

Thus was born the Sri Chinmoy Marathon Team: a non-profit organization set up by his disciples to promote fitness, well-being, foster a higher consciousness, and provide ample opportunity for self-transcendence. You could pick your limits: anywhere from a two-mile race held weekly for the public in Centres all over the world, to ultra long distance races in the thousands of miles range. My hat is off to any human who participates in these mind-blowing, "can a body really do that?" running events.

I learned quickly how rewarding self-transcendence was. Less than a year on the path I decided to run my first marathon. I was twenty-one. With no training, other than running two miles intermittently over the preceding months, I enthusiastically jumped into the race. Luckily, it was a completely flat course that ran the length of Silver Strand in Coronado near San Diego. I took the opportunity to practice what I'd learned over those months and focused on my heart. When my legs got tired I just focused with more intensity. I ended up with a 4:15 marathon time, which was about the same time I would complete many subsequent, but hillier, marathons for which I had done extensive training.

The sense of accomplishment was contagious to the other parts of my being. It gave me the confidence and showed me the inner strength to take on formidable challenges.

That marathon was the first of 25 marathons I would eventually run: many of them where the New York Marathon. But my best time came from what I consider to be my most soulfully run event. I was trained, the course was flat, and I was virtually pain-free, finishing in my best time of 3:35.

But more than completing these marathons was the discipline I gained from training for them. When I first started running I flat out hated it. I felt like a lead weight plodding the ground. With persistence, that totally changed into a real love of the sport. Now I don't even think of the pounding steps before I run. All I envision is fresh air, birds, sky, and the freeing feeling of moving forward through space. It's a chance to go inward and forward at the same time, feeling my connectedness with all that surrounds me.

My early years on the path were filled with physical activities. During my first six years I ran three marathons a year, completed biathlons, swimming races, and even did a few ultra-marathon events: a 12-hour running race in which I covered 60 miles, and few 47-mile races.

All these events gave me the confidence and willingness to embark on the biggest trek of my life in the years to come. They also instilled in me a real passion for fitness. It felt so good to be strong and to push the limits of my body and mind.

Every year, in August, the students of Sri Chinmoy from all over the world gathered in New York. Guru chose to live there so he could offer meditations at the United Nations, which he has done so, voluntarily, for over thirty years. Students came to celebrate Guru's birthday, August 27th. For two weeks of "Celebrations", as we called them, members of the worldwide Meditation Centres would put on performances of Guru's plays, poetry and music. There were walking meditations, silent meditations, sporting events and relaxing time cutting jokes and playing games. We even put on a circus and a parade, but participating in the 100-meter sprints was the highlight.

One of my favorite sporting events was our version of the Olympics called Sports Day. It was during the sprints that the Master's mysterious ways again became very evident to me. My favorite moment was when Guru would place the faster group of runners in heats. If we knew we were pretty good at sprints then we would let the slower girls place themselves in heats first, as the faster girls waited to be placed by Guru. Guru then created the last remaining heats by placing girls of similar capacity together. He simply knew. It was uncanny how we were so evenly placed. It made for very exciting races, as we were all neck and neck in the last few heats. I had the privilege of being placed in the last heat many times. It was inspiring to know someone had such confidence in my ability. It made me really want to train for sprinting because I was being shown that I had the capacity to do it well.

Sri Chinmoy also loves sprinting and was a decathlon champion in his youth.

Sprinting also offered me some intensely powerful spiritual experiences. One time, I was standing behind the other girls who were about to run, waiting my turn, when I found myself entering into an unbelievably high meditation. Even though I was trying to meditate, I was surprised how easy it was. There was no pre-race anxiety or fear whatsoever. I could see my Guru standing at the finish line and all I could feel was that I was about to blast off at top speed and, like a rocket, enter into the ocean of his consciousness. Gratitude prevailed and at the same time I felt inundated with love. The combination sent tears pouring from my eyes the moment the starting gun shot out. I was sprinting and crying at the same time.

What a gift! Time after time I received these jewels of inner experience; always in silence, no one knowing but my Guru and me what was going on. At times, I had to remind myself of how sacred and special those silent moments of connectedness were with my Guru.

If you allowed it, it was all too easy for your mind to convince you that your Guru didn't care about you if you focused on the outer attention he gave other disciples. This was a lethal trap for many disciples. One thing is clear on a spiritual path with a living Master: you will never understand with your mind why a Master says or does what he does; why he shows so much attention to someone else and not to you.

If you allow those thoughts to take over, you suffer miserably. I saw many disciples leave Guru's spiritual path because they were unable to allow him to do things his way. It's hard, when his way is sometimes incomprehensible. It's why faith in one's Guru is so important. If you can't have faith that what a Guru does for you and for others is the right thing, then you shouldn't have one. That is, perhaps, why so few do. The ego is a huge obstacle for a spiritual seeker. I certainly saw mine smashed many times. Unfortunately, it's also very resilient.

"The easiest way to conquer ego is to offer gratitude to God."
- Sri Chinmoy

A great place to have one's ego smashed or, rather, to cultivate humility, is a disciple-run restaurant. My first year on the path included such an experience; one that I will always look upon with fond memories. It was my first real immersion with disciples.

Carlos Santana owned the restaurant and his sister-in-law managed it, as they were disciples of Sri Chinmoy during my early years. But Guru was the ultimate boss, with the final word about important matters. He decided who could work there or who would be asked to leave. If you were fired it was usually due to violating one of Guru's strictest standards: no flirting with the opposite sex.

Even in a non-disciple workplace workers who indulge in sexual innuendos can suffer the same fate. Guru wanted boys and girls to work together like brothers and sisters. We were all striving to strengthen our connection with the Supreme. To have someone deliberately interrupt that process with his or her own sexual desires and attractions was a real violation. As a young and somewhat cute girl, I had a lion's share of those violations. And, admittedly, I liked it. It's always flattering to have a guy think you're attractive. But, by accepting Sri Chinmoy as my Guru I was shutting the door to that world at the age of 21, at least for as long as I could stand it.

Celibacy was a goal to strive for on Guru's path, even if you were married. Some reached it sooner than others. Whenever I taught meditation classes, this was always the topic of greatest consternation. Some people simply refused to entertain the possibility that a life of celibacy would be of assistance to one's spiritual progress, always arguing, "But what could be more beautiful than the love between a man and a woman expressed physically?" My answer was always the same: it depends on what you want. Certainly you can learn to meditate without being celibate, but can you remain in a high consciousness without being disturbed by the pull of sex day in and day out? Most men I've met think about sex a lot of the time. What we focus on we give strength to. So if our goal is to grow into our own highest consciousness, to move in the direction of greater Light, and remain there, why purposefully add a force that takes us farther from that goal? It's like shooting yourself in the foot while running for a touchdown.

The truth is, sexual urges automatically decrease when a focus is put on the heart's Light. Little by little, and with regular practice, the urge simply fades. I feel for men on this matter. In general, it's a much bigger hurdle for them than it is for women.

What women seem to suffer from is an insecurity that creates a need to have one's beauty validated. In other words, most women need to be cute, getting pleasure from making men feel their sex drive. We force each other down without even realizing it. Focusing on our spiritual attributes eventually puts an end to this downward spiral.

My struggle as a disciple was not about sex, but about companionship. I'm not an extroverted, social person. What I enjoy most is the company of one other person and the balance of a male energy. So this was by far the biggest struggle of my disciple life.

An Unconventional Pursuit

To alleviate this need I broke up with my boyfriend, who I had been with when I became a disciple, and moved into an apartment with two other disciple girls. I now lived and worked with disciples, participating in all the Centre activities. The outer world I once new quickly faded. I was now fully immersed in the spiritual life, and only in my first year on the path.

Sharing a room with another disciple proved to be more challenging than I imagined. Her name was Robin. We lived in a one-bedroom apartment with another disciple residing in the living room: too little personal space for someone like myself. The worst part was that Robin always seemed to be in competition with me - looking to see who was being more soulful, who meditated longer, who had more devotion and the list went on. I found it maddening. Looking back, I realize I was having my first encounter with a fanatical disciple; not someone I wanted to emulate. She hadn't been on the path much longer than I had, so she was easy to dismiss. Luckily, there were many others who did fuel my inspiration.

Living with her taught me an early lesson in not judging the Master by the disciple. I learned to discriminate who to spend time with and who to leave alone. My need to be around genuine people became much more pronounced on the path. I saw a very reasonable Master who had some very fanatical disciples, but certainly not all. Many of Guru's disciples are the most amazing individuals I ever met. They carry the Master's Light and his mission to the heights it deserves.

*Character is just what we
Inwardly are and outwardly do.*

- Sri Chinmoy

Besides the torture of burning, crying eyes from preparing onions for the chopper everyday, my strongest memories of the restaurant involve the disciples and the customers. After a very early morning of food preparation my job was to serve the customers in a cafeteria-style arrangement.

The restaurant, then called Dipti Nivas, was a vegetarian haven for the diverse population of the lower Castro area of San Francisco. One man, who came in regularly, made up half his face so he looked half man, half woman, complete with one false eyelash. Seeing him always sent a shiver up my spine. But what truly moved me was the reaction people of every background had to that establishment. For them it was a temple: a haven of peace amidst the city's confusion. And it's not that it was quiet, far from it. There was a line out the door everyday, with every seat filled. The dynamic energy in that place rivaled Beethoven's best symphonies. The prayerful and meditative energy consciously put forth by the workers, from morning to night, created the soulful consciousness that permeated Dipti Nivas and touched everyone who entered its doors; the Master's Light percolated throughout. Many felt it.

As a matter of fact, when Carlos Santana left Guru's path and Dipti Nivas along with its recipes was sold, the clientele drastically reduced. The new restaurant called Amazing Grace served much of the same food, but without the same consciousness people just weren't as attracted.

I was seeing for myself the powerful impact of a higher consciousness on humanity. It made me proud to be a part of that transformation. For the first time in my life I felt like I was doing something truly useful for the betterment of the world. It made me want to do more. My sense of purpose was rapidly growing.

The customers weren't my only inspiration. Observing the other disciples was equally impressive. I was struck by the discipline so many workers displayed. I'd often go back into the kitchen, a room filled with a half dozen workers, and it would be void of talking. All I could hear were the sounds of their work tempered by Sri Chinmoy's music. That was another of Guru's requests: not to talk while working so you could remain in a meditative consciousness. No doubt, it added to the deliciousness of the food. The silence of Dipti Nivas's kitchen was such a contrast to the kitchens of many bustling restaurants, where yelling and cursing are the norm.

Then there was Dharana. Bless her heart. I'll never forget the awe with which I was struck as I'd watch this girl work the cash register. With every spare moment she'd write the word Supreme on a piece of paper near the register. Even when we were really busy she'd be writing in the moments between customers.

That's what I loved about my early years in San Francisco. The disciples gave their all to their spiritual lives. I'd never witnessed such intensity within a group of people. And unfortunately, I'd never witness it again; for being a part of such a talented, disciplined and powerful group of people was an unparalleled experience. I was especially in awe of the musical talent. Along with Carlos Santana there was a future Grammy winner and inspirational drummer, Narada Michael Walden, plus a dozen other extremely talented musicians. In that Centre, if my meditation didn't carry me up the musical performances certainly did.

After a long, hard week at the restaurant most of us spent our weekends putting on activities for the public. Almost every weekend was something different: manning an aid station for a running race, singing with a group of girls for a public concert, attending a meditation class by another disciple, or putting up flyers on the streets of San Francisco to advertise one of these events. And since Guru felt that spirituality should not have a price tag there was plenty of fund raising as well, like baking and selling mass quantities of cookies. A nice benefit of participating in these public events was that I had great meditations, and, at the same time, I could contribute to giving others the opportunity to have one too. Years later, when I conducted my own meditation classes, I would have some of the best meditations of my life while teaching others how to meditate.

It really didn't matter what I was doing in that first year. I was so pumped up about the life I was leading: everything was new, my heart was being fed daily, and everyday was filled with discoveries. I learned more about myself and my strengths and weaknesses than in all the years before. I was learning to see people as evolving souls to feel compassion for and oneness with, rather than to judge. And I was just beginning to create a connection with my Master that would never stop developing.

Inner awareness brings
Enthusiasm and enthusiasm
Brings inner awareness.

-Sri Chinmoy

What was becoming very clear about that connection was the stark difference between the inner and outer relationship.

Now, many years later and no longer on the path, I am reaping the benefits of having strengthened that inner connection. I thank the Master for that, for over all the years I spent as an active member of the Meditation Centre I received very little outer attention from him. I didn't become dependent on it, though I sure wished it would come. Now I'm glad it didn't. By not receiving attention I was compelled to focus inwardly with more intensity. Whenever I did so my Master's love and concern were right there waiting for me. At times, the feeling was overwhelming and tears just poured from my eyes while meditating. Those moments taught me that no form of outer attention could ever equal the sublime beauty of an inner experience of one's Master. I could relate countless examples. They come to my memory like a torrential flood, each one unique to the other; like the time I sat in the front row just feet from my Guru in the Los Angeles airport.

We were taking prasad, or blessed food, from the Master. My mother came along that day and she was ahead of me in line. Guru spoke, "Ah, you are the mother of Kent and Lynn," beaming an ear-to-ear smile at her. When it was my turn he spoke again (a rare occurrence for me) and commented with a tone of amazement on how much I looked like my mother. I responded, jokingly, by saying, "Thank God it's her and not my brother that I look just like!" My brother is practically bald. Guru just smiled and was on to the next disciple.

I returned to my seat feeling such a sense of delight for having that light-hearted interchange with my Guru. Then the thought flashed through my mind that Guru probably didn't think it was very funny. I wondered if, perhaps, it was inappropriate of me to joke with him, since the look on his face became so serious when the next disciple stood before him. And almost as fast as that thought struck my mind I felt Guru's laughter inside my heart. Outwardly I was looking at a serious expression, but inwardly we were laughing together at the joke. There was almost a giddy feeling, akin to a child's squeals of delight while playing, going on inside me and it lasted a very long time. Basically, I was cracking up in my seat and on an inner plane Guru was cracking up with me. He even quickly glanced over to me and smiled right in the middle of another serious confrontation with another disciple, as if outwardly acknowledging that he could feel my humorous state.

My mother, on the other hand, was blown away in the seat next to me. I could tell by her stillness and the energy she was putting out. She was feeling the mind-blowing effects of Guru's blessings and Light.

Sitting on my other side was a dear friend who was having her own unique experience, practically crying out-loud. I could hear her sobbing, and they weren't tears of joy. I thought to myself, "Wow, Guru is witnessing a room full of as many different experiences as there were people, and fully present for each of us on a personal level." I cannot even imagine what his world must be like.

On another occasion, during a visit to New York, I was meditating at what Guru calls Aspiration Ground: an outdoor tennis court with bleacher-like seating for the disciples. It's as versatile as it is uplifting: a place not only used for playing tennis (one of Guru's favorite sports), but also as the grounds for many celebrations, such as the day we honored Guru's mother's 100 year centenary. This particular story took place while Guru was seated and talking with another disciple. My mind cooperated that day and stayed quiet enough for me to enter a really powerful meditation. During that meditation I was overwhelmed with higher emotions. The sense of gratitude pervaded every cell of my body. As I gazed at my Guru it felt as if the whole world had disappeared, yet I was vividly cognizant of it. It was like having a keen awareness of two worlds at the same time. Love poured into and out of me, dancing with tears of gratitude like some divine choreography. It was as if every emotion that was sent forth from my heart came back to me ten fold. I was on the threshold of the unknown, feeling I would surely cross over it if just one more drop of love entered into me. I was communing with my Guru deeper than ever, as he sat there in conversation. Then he suddenly looked straight up at me - the other disciple still talking to him - and I felt his acknowledgement. He kept looking. His gaze fixed on my eyes as he outwardly entered a meditation, his eyes revealing the shift from conversation to meditation.

The tiny drop had entered the vast ocean of her Guru's consciousness again. And again I wished I could stay there forever. That love surpassed any love I ever felt with another human being. It was divine love, utterly freeing and utterly fulfilling.

Guru would say that the closest thing to divine love was the human love of a mother for her child, but that even that was no comparison.

Then I saw movement in the periphery of my vision. I glanced down and saw a girl sitting just below and to the side of me, starring at my face as my tears poured down. She was looking to see whom Guru was meditating on, and the look on my face must have captivated her. She smiled at me and I knew she was acknowledging what I was experiencing. She was one of those amazing older disciples who, undoubtedly, had her fair share of what I was experiencing. Then, gradually, it ended and Guru returned to his conversation.

This was a clear example for me of how Guru is able to operate on many levels at the same time. When I returned to a somewhat normal consciousness I glanced to my left and saw the three girls next to me all asleep; heads practically in their laps. I looked to my right and saw the same thing. The flash of mental doubt that sometimes seems to pop up after I see Guru looking at me was easily destroyed, for I had wondered, afterward, if he was really looking at me. It surprised me that I even had the thought given the magnitude of that inner experience. No wonder the world is a mess, given most of humanity is governed by the mind with all its doubt and confusion.

I could probably fill a book just with these experiences. I was fortunate, though my mind certainly didn't always believe that; for the attention I got, usually of an inner nature, was much deeper, more intense, and more personal than any words Guru could tell me. It was something I had to constantly remind myself of.

One of the ways Guru appeased everyone's need for some outer recognition was through phone calls. Since I was fortunate enough to be a member of one of Guru's premier Centres, phone conversations were common, but not so common that we weren't delighted when it rang. The intervals between phone calls seemed perfectly timed. He even called the Dipti Nivas restaurant and talked to all the workers from time to time. It was always a thrill and always revealed to me where my consciousness was at, since I immediately tried to elevate it the moment the phone rang.

There were two phone conversations that stood out during my early years on the path. In one, Guru asked me whom my Centre leader was, as I had just moved from San Francisco to San Diego, although when he called I was visiting the San Francisco Centre.

Every Meditation Centre has a leader assigned by Guru to lead the meditations, deliver messages between the disciples and Guru, and make decisions regarding the Centre. Other than Centre leaders, there is primarily only one person through whom all messages get delivered. His name is Ashrita. The same person who holds the greatest number of Guinness records, clearly holds the record for delivering messages between a Master and his disciples.

When I replied to Guru that my Centre leader's name was John he responded, "John? John who?" I answered, "John Savage," and Guru howled with laughter. I didn't see what was so funny. Then he said, "No, no, no, not John Savage, it's John the Baptist!"

Well, I was sure Guru had a reason for telling me that, so I just replied, "Oh Guru, my mistake, you're right, it is John the Baptist." Guru just thought that was hysterical and cracked up again.

It was delightful to hear Guru laugh so loudly, but the exchange left me wondering why he said it and why to me? I do distinctly remember him saying that there is an element of truth to every joke. So I couldn't help but wonder if my Centre leader had an incarnation as that esteemed personage. There certainly were plenty of parallels.

John, later given the spiritual name Mahiyan, meaning nobility, was the only one in a group of 50 new disciples who insisted that Guru was a realized Master when a very charismatic, older disciple declared himself to be the Master that everyone should follow, and that Sri Chinmoy had lost his Light.

I had the opportunity to witness that unimaginable moment, as I had just happened to be visiting San Diego at the time. It's one of the juiciest stories tucked in the memory book of my past.

> *Since you have learned so well*
> *The art of deceiving others,*
> *I am sure you will perfect your art*
> *Until you can deceive yourself as well.*
>
> *-Sri Chinmoy*

Still in the first year of my discipleship, with just a glimmer of who Guru was, it was easy to believe the convincing anecdotes of Fred Lenz. Fred, given the spiritual name Atmananda, but whom I will refer to as Fred since he no longer deserves such an exalted name, had earned everyone's trust, respect and admiration. Everyone, meaning the 50 seekers he brought to Guru's path through his incredibly funny and captivating spiritual talks. It was in Fred's meditation class that I had my first heart-center experience. A part of me will always feel a sense of gratitude to him for bringing me my Guru.

Fred made spirituality fun. He'd often make references to Carlos Castanada and take us out to the beaches of La Jolla Shores to dabble in all kinds of occult activities, like doing the "gate of power". I later learned that Guru was totally against dabbling in the occult. Fred, himself, seemed to have some occult power. He used it that eventful night. It was a sensation I'll never forget. Luckily I had already experienced my heart-center opening. I knew just what that felt like. It gave me a basis with which to compare the occult experience I had with Fred.

One night, we all met to meditate as usual. But then the unusual happened. Fred sat in front of us instead of a picture of our Guru and convinced us with anecdotal stories that our Guru had lost his Light. He told us to meditate on him instead. One by one he looked at each person as we meditated. When his eyes locked on mine I suddenly felt the most unusual sensation.

It was as if something grabbed my heart and pulled it upward with a quick jerk. I have never felt anything like it. It was an exciting sensation, like something inside me had been temporarily activated. The experience was nothing like the time I first tried meditation, with the abiding sense of peace that emulated from the expanding, rotating warmth. And it left me with no feeling of wanting to remain in that state forever, like I had many times with Guru after this. Instead, it felt jarring, with no lasting effects. But the fact that this man had clearly done it to me, and that it was so unusual and in the same area as my heart-center, was very convincing. If it had happened today I would have known it was just the play of occult power. But with so few inner experiences I had little reason to disbelieve him.

Luckily, I had to return to my college studies. So back to San Francisco I went, hearing how this drama played out through conversations with my brother who had also been present that night.

It was "John the Baptist", alone, who refused to accept Fred's proclamation. He tried to convince others to stay with Guru. Only six out of the 50 present did. One of them was my brother, Kent, later given the spiritual name Gochar.

Fred soon moved his following to another location and quickly grew its numbers, charging hundreds of dollars to his followers: something Guru told us was a clear sign of a false Master. In the end, many years later, Fred's body was found drowned in the ocean. He had overdosed on drugs.

> *Do not kill yourself worrying*
> *About false teachers.*
> *Your sincerity-shield*
> *Will protect you and also definitely*
> *Help you find a real teacher.*
>
> *– Sri Chinmoy*

I was left wondering about another phone call that happened in that first year. I was working at Dipti Nivas. In that call Guru told me I was the link between the California Centres. Upon hearing it I was a bit bewildered. What did it mean? I was so new to the path and had only really become a disciple through the San Diego Meditation Centre with a few subsequent visits. So to be referred to as the link was a little amazing to me.

Of course, as with most things Guru says, they eventually make perfect sense. As the years passed I found myself yearning to bring the various Centres together. I would choreograph all kinds of wacky performances that included the members of all the California Centres.

Every year, as part of Guru's birthday celebrations, the disciples from all over the world would put on a circus. It was a private function, not open for public viewing. The acts would start after noon and go on until the early hours of the morning. It was one of my favorite functions, and the perfect venue for a humorous act involving all the California disciples.

It was at the end of one of these circuses that Guru caught me by surprise. He was handing out a bag filled with prasad to everyone present. When my turn came Guru held onto the bag and meditated on me. He then opened it up and meditated on its contents before handing me the bag. I felt Guru's gratitude pour into me, and by the time I returned to my seat I felt like a light bulb about to explode from over-wattage. It was a clear acknowledgment that my efforts to unite California were significant. I was doing what I was meant to do. On another occasion I created a circus act that ended in a song I wrote about California. I took most of the words from a lecture Guru once gave on the qualities of our state and put it to music. The next day the Center leader of San Francisco approached me saying that Guru was softly singing my song while seated at his chair. By that evening Guru had written his own California song and taught it to the California disciples, asking us to sing it whenever we all got together. Needless to say, that song always strikes a cord deep in my heart that fills me with inspiration and admiration for our exquisite state. For me, California is the guiding light of our country.

When I think back to all the circuses I had seen, my whole being smiles. I had some of my heartiest laughs watching those acts. Guru asked us to do them because it brought forward childlike, innocent joy. And having childlike joy was at the core of Sri Chinmoy's philosophy. Peace, love and joy create an unimaginably powerful strength. They have existed in every Master that walked the earth, and learning to cultivate them has remained the foundation of their teachings.

Guru would weave joy into every activity. He even said it could be used to measure whether a particular spiritual teacher was right for you. If an idea is followed by joy (not pleasure) then, he said, follow it. Always let joy be your guide. Of course, one first has to be cognizant of the difference between pleasure and joy. Pleasure gives us the feeling of indulgence, where joy feels expansive. Joy seems to move out from us, like ripples in water, touching everyone in its wake. Consequently, to feel joy is to offer joy. It cannot help but be given away. It is even in Guru's definition of humility.

It was joy that permeated my early years. It would spring unexpectedly from almost anything, and of course, it was in humor too. There was so much humor on Guru's path that it was practically like being in some divine comedy club. I have uncountable recollections of flopping back in my chair while in the room with Guru saying to myself, "God, he's funny!" It seems that anyone whoever does reach the exalted point of conversing with God would surely leave laughing.

Monty Python aptly portrayed this wisdom in a song called, "Always Look on the Bright Side of Life." My favorite line is: "When life is jolly rotten there's something you've forgotten, and that's to laugh and smile and dance and sing."

As a teacher I even had my fifth graders sing this song whenever someone got in a bad mood. No wonder Guru liked to watch Monty Python.

Look for perfection in others.
Your very search will give you
Abundant joy.
Look for perfection inside your nature.
Your very search will awaken you
To love perfection evermore.

– Sri Chinmoy

All the experiences of innocent joy over the years have made finding it second nature. I feel it for the simplest of things: the way a cat walks, the shape of a cloud, fruit trees; it may well be the greatest gift I have been given. Unfortunately, when something with light becomes even brighter, things of darkness seem even darker. I am often amazed at the crudeness with which people express humor or have fun. Drinking alcohol and getting drunk have been equated with having a good time for as long as I can remember. We are constantly being misled. Too many of us simply do not know where to find joy. It's been so confused with pleasure that we don't even know the difference.

On a spiritual path feeling joy is especially crucial. The task of a seeker is long and arduous. We are constantly faced with making choices between things of lesser or greater light. The responsibility to strive for an ever-higher standard in the face of tremendous forces that want to pull us farther from our goal can be overwhelming.

As I practiced meditation I saw myself with more clarity: the good and the bad. I discovered goodness I didn't know was there, like the ability to feel intense gratitude in an instant. But, oh the weaknesses, when they showed their ugly faces joy was far away. Guru would repeatedly encourage us to cheerfully accept ourselves with the view to transformation, but it wasn't easy.

An Unconventional Pursuit

> *Depression is not the answer*
> *Suppression is not the answer*
> *Rejection is not the answer*
> *Illumination is the inner answer*
> *Transformation is the outer answer*
>
> *– Sri Chinmoy*

There was one time in particular when Guru seemed to be showing us the importance of cultivating this virtue. He called for an abs contest, asking all the boys to line up and, one by one, stand in front of him with their shirts lifted above their abs. He then gave each boy a mark between one and a hundred. As with everything the Master does, this event was rich in lessons. Egos were smashed, humility was crowned, and everyone present experienced the art of cheerful self-acceptance, even as a spectator. For some, Guru turned what could have been an embarrassing display of lumps and bulges into an opportunity to laugh at ourselves, and, at the same time, become inspired to improve. It is a real art. When we become masters of this art, joy and happiness reign.

Then there was the time I laughed so hard I couldn't see straight. I was watching one of those infamous circus acts. Guru had recently announced that there should be no more dancing acts with one exception: fat boys can dance. Dancing fat boys, it seems, don't display sexual, vital energy. But, as I witnessed, they do display unprecedented humor.

A group of boys put together a contest, asking for volunteers to stand, straight-faced, in front of the next act. If they laughed or even cracked a smile they were out of the competition. Whoever remained unswerved by the hysterics before them was the winner.

One by one the boys of discipline stepped down from the bleachers to test their long-practiced self-control. The powerhouses, like Ashrita, Mahiyan and others, took on the challenge. I watched them fervently putting themselves into a meditative, detached consciousness as they awaited their test.

Then beautiful, classical music pulsed through the air and with it came a dozen of the fattest boys on the path, adorned like ballerinas, complete with tights and tutus, flitting through the air and delicately pounding on their toes. It was beautifully choreographed, gracefully executed and uproariously funny; something akin to a Monty Python skit and most probably conjured up by the British disciples. No wonder Guru said fat boys can dance. Unfortunately, I can't tell you who won. I simply can't remember, probably because I was laughing so uncontrollably.

I miss those precious moments on the path. It's hard to find that combination of joy, humor and purity displayed in the world around me. Perhaps one of the closest examples was a Tim Conway sketch I once saw on the Carol Burnett Show when he was carrying a fire hose at a snail's pace.

Unfortunately, as the years progressed, it became harder to feel joy on the path. It became clouded by my mind's revolt. I allowed what I didn't like to take precedence. We see what we focus on, and since I was focused on what I lacked, that is what I saw. In fact, it consumed me, and left joy in the dust.

Many of Guru's aphorisms refer to the importance of experiencing newness. Newness is what made my early years on the path so joyful. It is no wonder that children are filled with this quality. Guru urged us to cultivate newness in our daily lives, insisting that it would keep our spiritual aspiration strong. I can now say I'm a living example of this truth.

> *Do you know the secret of my Spiritual success?*
> *I have freed myself from the past.*
> *I live in the constant, unending Newness of life.*
>
> – Sri Chinmoy

Although phone calls from Guru were common, for me conversations with him in person were very rare. The first time it happened was surprising. I was visiting New York for my first "Celebrations" experience. I was just under one year on the path. There was a very long line of disciples waiting to take prasad and I was near the end of it. My eyes were closed in meditation as I prepared myself for those few special moments when each of us has a one-on-one experience of our Master. Actually, it was more like a desperate attempt to calm my nerves so I wasn't a complete wreck before my turn came.

Suddenly, my roommate awakened me from my nervous trance. Shaking my arm, she frantically called out, "Guru wants to see you!" A wave of shock washed over me. Before I knew it I was standing in front of my Master as he looked at me with those meditative eyes that seem to be saying, "I know everything about you." It was a beautifully strange feeling, standing before my Guru. My nervousness dissolved into a pool of sweetness and love. It felt like Guru was seeing a person of great potential. I'm sure he sees that in everyone, but in that moment I truly felt it.

To have someone look at you and silently convey that you have tremendous potential is unbelievably uplifting. Guru joked at first, then proceeded to tell me that I needed to lose weight. I heard a few gasps from some fat girls standing near enough to hear Guru speak. But I felt no embarrassment at all. I was 15 or 20 pounds overweight. So for Guru to acknowledge that showed me how intensely my weight affected my consciousness and my performance.

Apparently, I wasn't alone. According to Guru, being overweight even by a few pounds enormously affects the consciousness of girls. Boys, however, are impacted far less.

I did eventually lose that weight. I finally acquired the poise and discipline towards eating that I lacked in my youth. Now I'm not only more fit, but I've offered consultations in nutrition and weight loss to others. I owe my understanding of health and fitness to my Guru. It was his example and his philosophy of an integral approach to spiritual growth that allowed me to see the impact the physical and spiritual have on one another. It helped, too, that after many years on his path Guru asked me and my former husband to open a health food store: an experience that greatly contributed to my knowledge of health. Unfortunately, it was also the beginning of the end of my life as a disciple.

Change yourself slowly
And cheerfully.
Conditions will change immediately
And unimaginably.
   – Sri Chinmoy

Although my early years were a time of great enthusiasm and joy, I had my share of challenges too. Like many spiritual seekers, finding a path and a teacher also meant receiving tremendous opposition from family members. I couldn't blame them. It took me a full year to see the value of a spiritual teacher.

My parents hoped my brother and I were going through some kind of phase. They feared we were a part of some dark group that would warp our minds. But my experience of Sri Chinmoy and the activities we participated in could not be refuted. Charismatic, false teachers exist. But so do genuine Masters and genuine spiritual paths. Light and darkness will probably always exist together, but, so too will the heart's wisdom. What is important is to be sincere. A truly sincere hunger for the spiritual life is bound to lead a seeker to a sincere path.

As the years progressed and my parents began to meet the other disciples and hear of our activities they gained respect for Guru and his mission; although, they never could get themselves to call my brother and I by our spiritual names.

Having a brother on the same path was a real boon. We supported each other through the trials and joys. Also, it was like having double the experiences. His accomplishments felt like mine. When he would travel with Guru to a foreign country, to some extent, so did I. But my most favorite shared experience was when Gochar would play music.

The name, Gochar, means the seeker who manifests the Supreme through all the senses. To know him is to see the real validity of this name. But it was while manifesting the Supreme through the sense of hearing that most people witnessed the meaning of his name. He has many fans, but I am his greatest.

An Unconventional Pursuit

As kids, Gochar and I began piano lessons at an early age: too early for me. I quit after two years and proceeded to forget everything I learned. But Gochar stayed with it and took his skill to a spiritual level.

Our Centre leader in San Diego, Mahiyan, would often ask Gochar to play his arrangements of Sri Chinmoy's melodies on the piano while everyone meditated. It always intensified my meditations. And if I couldn't meditate it simply took me there. We all adored his music. I loved it so much that I'd often stand next to the piano in full admiration and watch him play, wishing I would create those elevating sounds.

One day, seated at the piano at my parent's home, I sat and meditated. I wanted so much to feel the satisfaction of creating soulful music. I saw on my brother's face that when he played he was transported to a higher consciousness. It compelled me to make the attempt. I couldn't read even the simplest of melodies, so I figured one out by ear. Then, keeping my mind completely out of the process, I added my left hand. Before I knew it I was playing my own soulful arrangement of Guru's music.

To a trained musician it probably sounded like junk, but to my ears it was heaven. I soon found myself spending hours at the piano, plucking out melodies by ear that stilled my mind and opened my heart. I found a new love.

Since then I've been complemented many times while playing the piano. For me it is clearly the power of identification. When we meditate we identify with the object of our concentration. It enters into us and becomes a part of our consciousness. This was much like the ease with which I learned to study while in college. I identified with my brother's talent and a part of it became my own.

The power of identification is another reason why having a spiritual Master expedites our progress. When we meditate on a Master we are identifying with a higher consciousness. It then enters into us and becomes our own. All disciples of spiritual Masters carry their Master's Light to some degree. The stronger the identification, the stronger is the Light.

After 20 years on the path this phenomenon was poignantly pointed out one day while I was working in my health food store. I was standing at the register looking out the window when I saw a man walking toward my store. Sri Chinmoy's name was not visible from the outside of the store, and only in very fine print, if you looked in the right place, on the inside. When the customer entered he headed straight toward me without looking around and asked for a bottle of vitamin C. No sooner than we had made the exchange, did he look right into my eyes and declare, "You're a student of Sri Chinmoy." A bit surprised by his swift skill I responded, "Yes, how did you know? Is it because I'm wearing a sari?" He confidently and a bit proudly for nailing it on the head, replied, "No, I just know. I've read the books of many Masters and I can feel each one's unique Light, and you have Sri Chinmoy's Light." He then related to me many incidences of telling people who their Guru was, always nailing it precisely.

True or not, that customer sure made me feel good. To know that my Guru's Light was in me strong enough to be detected by a complete stranger was very encouraging. Progress has been made. I hope that even though I have now left Sri Chinmoy's path that his Light still remains with me.

CHAPTER FOUR
EMBRACING THE WORLD

The years passed quickly, and the path was changing as much as I was. The numbers of disciples from all over the world was rapidly increasing. And they all wanted to come to New York. Luckily I got to witness the path when there were still relatively few students. The meeting rooms were smaller and more intimate, prasad was often handed or thrown directly to us from Guru, and the faces I'd see during Celebrations were usually familiar ones.

That was the beauty of Guru's global path. Twice a year his students met in New York to celebrate his birthday on August 27th, and the day Guru came to America, which was April 13th. It was like traveling the world without leaving New York. I made good friends from all over the world. And those that weren't good friends were familiar faces that always gave me joy. I had a second family and it was huge. Guru brought the world together on his path and it gave each of us the opportunity to feel our oneness with humanity.

The unique spiritual qualities of each country showed through its disciples when they performed. The Japanese were incredibly soulful, the British were either very precise or totally hysterical, the German performances were always powerful, and the Africans revealed such humility, simplicity and beauty. Many of Guru's disciples couldn't afford the flight to New York, so Guru would ask the Centres that could to raise money to bring them. Guru himself would often pay for his disciples to come. One time he even handed my former husband $500 so he could go to New York. I remember we even gathered running shoes from the American Centres to send to the Russian disciples so they could run. "Unity in multiplicity" is what Guru would say about the goal of humanity, and his path was a microcosm for that goal.

Sometimes we succeeded in it, but at other times we definitely failed. I certainly had a hard time with a few German girls who still seemed to uphold the motto of the master race. One girl even went so far as to remove my things from my chair and claim it as her own. You have to understand, getting a seat at a function in New York during Celebrations is no easy task.

But when we were at our best, it was really good. One of my favorite memories of our global family being soulful was on Christmas Eve. Christmas was never celebrated with a tree and presents; instead, we would meditate and sing, sometimes for seven hours. The first time I participated in a Christmas celebration in New York was early on. It's lucky too; as these New York functions soon vanished when Guru started extending his winter travels.

We started at midnight, and for seven hours we sang bajans (short songs that are repeated several times). Guru has written thousands of songs, but the bajans we sang on Christmas were about Christ, Krishna, the Buddha and other spiritual Masters.

I loved that night. We all sat facing a stage adorned with seven shrines for seven Masters with Christ in the middle. The only break in the music was at the end of each hour when we took prasad. Hour by hour the room slowly thinned out. Guru had left the room shortly after we started singing, but returned in the early morning hours. It was about 4 am when he appeared again. Guru praised us for staying with it and handed each of us prasad. I thought to myself, "This must be what heaven is like." The sense of peace was profound. The candles, incense and tiny white lights that adorned the Indian setting on the stage were ethereal. I wished it was forever rather than seven hours. Though my body struggled at times to stay awake, its need for sleep surrendered to the force of my inner cry for divinity. My heart's devotion to the inner life was on fire as I bathed in Light. I was not raised a Christian, my mother is Jewish, although I did attend a few church services at the invitation of friends. Yet, that night, for the first time in my life, I actually felt Christ's presence. And ever since then a connection with Christ has existed. Christmas was forever changed.

Seeing how devoid of spirituality Christmas has become in our country, with the material world taking precedence over devotion, has completely turned me off to celebrating it in the traditional way. Singing traditional Christmas songs feels just plain silly.

Christ wasn't the only Master Guru's path brought me closer to. Krishna, the Buddha, Ramakrishna and Sri Aurobindo took on new life too. I had an incredibly intense experience of Krishna's consciousness while playing him in a performance. I had memorized lines from the *Gita* where Krishna was talking to Arjuna, his closest disciple, and put together a short play with a couple of other girls. As I played the role of Krishna I felt my own identity completely dissolve into his. For a few fleeting moments I was Krishna, or so it felt.

Sri Chinmoy opening the Parliament of the World's Religions with a meditation.

I even remember feeling that I had to step back into my own identity when I was done. Guru and the audience seemed to have had the same experience for we received an astounding ovation as Guru cheered, "Ba, ba, ba, excellent, excellent, excellent." So many boys and girls came up to me afterwards telling me how inspired they were by my performance. It was yet another one of those poignant moments when identifying with a higher consciousness left a lasting mark on my heart.

I had felt Christ's consciousness and I had felt Krishna's consciousness. Years later I would also feel the Buddha's. Really, this is just another example of how Guru showed all of us the beauty and necessity of oneness: oneness with humanity and oneness with humanity's diverse beliefs.

Opportunities to visit Guru in New York on Christmas changed as time passed. Each winter Guru and many of the disciples would travel to other countries. The experience was so loved by all that the time frame kept expanding. It's now up to over three months. From the middle of November to the middle of February, you can find Guru and hundreds of his disciples sharing in the special qualities other countries have to offer. After five years on the path, I made my first trip of this kind to Japan.

Sri Chinmoy with Nelson Mandela and New York City Mayor David Dinkins, 22 June 1990. Following were Sri Chinmoy's words to Mr. Mandela: *"South Africa sleeplessly needs the fragrance of your heart for its liberation and peace, and the whole world soulfully needs the garden of your life for its inspiration and bliss."*

Mikhail Gorbachev with Sri Chinmoy as he honors the Peace Run.

Traveling to foreign countries with a spiritual Master was a far cry from being a tourist. Wherever Guru went he met with the heads of state, often meditating with the country's leader. Since Guru has been voluntarily conducting meditations at the UN for over 30 years, some of these leaders were already familiar with him and offered lavish welcome ceremonies for Guru and his disciples. We would often watch as Guru lifted leaders and dignitaries over his head on a special platform.

Jigisha and I, like many disciples, also had the privilege of being lifted by Sri Chinmoy.

Always, Guru would compose a song for these people and a group of singers would honor them with it. As disciples we become a part of the Master's mission and all his undertakings. My 23 years as a disciple left me feeling connected to some degree with all the people Guru's Light has touched. Being a runner, one of my favorite connections was with Carl Lewis, the four-time Olympic gold medal winner in track and field.

One day, while in New York, Carl Lewis attended a function. Guru asked for the small singing group that I was a part of to take the stage and sing while Carl Lewis was there. I was so honored. By then, the power of identification was very real to me. I used to chant Carl Lewis's spiritual name, Sudahota, in silence, as I'd do running races. I even finished first in my fastest one-mile race ever when I chanted his name. My body identified with his speed and flew. For an average "Joe" of a runner that 5:50 mile was like lightening for me. I told Carl that story one day. He lit up, gave me a high five, and said it really touched him.

Another activity we usually did on these travels was to put on a free concert for the public. I remember being really impressed in Japan upon seeing the concert hall filled up for Guru's performance. Since it was my first trip abroad with Guru, I hadn't realized yet how much more receptive, open and soulful the rest of the world was compared to Americans. It seemed that every country I traveled to with Guru made the U.S.A. seem cruder, more ignorant, and more spiritually un-evolved as a whole.

Bali took first prize for the most prayerful and soulful people I had met. And it was so easy to spread the news of an upcoming concert or run for peace through the city streets. Wherever we went the media and the people treated us with such respect, gladly honoring our requests. By the time the concert started there was standing room only.

Many of Guru's disciples manage to join him every year on these trips. I had the chance to go on a handful. Each trip was unique. For example, in Maui we ran the perimeter of the island, starting at its highest point of Mount Haliakala. We visited schools all along the way and talked to the kids about how peace starts with each of us. Needless to say, I feel so much more connected to the Hawaiian culture now, as these kids so easily let us into their hearts.

Organizing these trips was a formidable undertaking, made even more remarkable by the individual who created them. Her name is Alo, and with the assistance of two disciples she traveled the world to make these "Christmas Trips" possible.

But Alo deserves credit for much more than organizing these global excursions. She was the individual who recognized Sri Chinmoy's height at the Sri Aurobindo Ashram, and was instrumental in bringing Guru to the West. In the end, she not only brought Guru to America but she brought him to the entire world.

I learned about her life with Guru from a phone call. It happened, one day, when unexpectedly Alo called my home. She wanted to thank my husband and I for a book we sent her about a western woman who lived with the Australian Aborigines.

She said she loved the story. It was especially poignant since Alo has a Master's Degree in cultural anthropology from the University of Toronto. It was her studies that led her to seek out work in India. Later she was a seeker at the Sri Aurobindo Ashram where she met Sri Chinmoy.

For twenty minutes I listened to the story of Alo's early years with Guru. I was fascinated and moved, for in that simple gesture Alo made me feel, for the first time, like a solid member of my Guru's spiritual family.

CHAPTER FIVE
THE FIRST PARTING

The opening of a disciple-run restaurant in San Diego called Jyoti Bihanga marked my 6th year on the path. It was quite an accomplishment for us as a Centre. We had been talking about it for years, then creating it for months. It is located on Adams Avenue in a part of San Diego that was, at the time, pretty undesirable. I'll never forget the Master's scolding to us about the selection of that location. At the time, our Meditation Centre was in La Jolla, a very upscale community, and we all wanted the restaurant to be located there. Our Centre leader, Mahiyan, sent the photos of several available sites. When Guru selected the Adams Avenue site we all begged Mahiyan to tell Guru what an awful neighborhood it was. He succumbed to our pressure and we got the slap of a lifetime. Guru's message was, "Those stupid fools! Don't they realize I have a vision?"

It was a real eye-opener for me. I realized in that response that even after six years on the path I still didn't put Guru in his proper place. It's so easy to forget that spiritual Masters see all, especially this one. Even the Master of the Sufi path, Pir Vilayat Khan, upon meeting Guru said, "I see, but you see all." That's quite a hefty compliment coming from one God-realized Master to another. We really are such fools from the spiritual point of view. And we are among the ones who are consciously pursuing perfection. That's scary.

> *He is an excellent spiritual teacher*
> *Whose eyes are firmness*
> *And whose heart is forgiveness.*
>
> *– Sri Chinmoy*

Our San Diego Meditation Centre was small at the time we opened the restaurant. There were, perhaps, a dozen of us who regularly attended the meditations and put on activities for the public. And even fewer committed themselves to working full-time at the restaurant. It was definitely a monetary sacrifice.

I had left teaching and let my college degree gather dust to become a waitress. You can be sure my parents heaved a heavy sigh. I wanted to learn about restaurants so I could contribute to creating our own. For six months I even temporarily moved back to San Francisco to train as a cook. That was, undoubtedly, one of the greatest skills I could have learned for me personally and for all those who would ever share a meal that I cooked. Guru's path has a way of expanding our abilities well beyond what we would have otherwise done. Not surprisingly, I also now teach cooking skills for better health.

By the time Jyoti Bihanga opened I was fully psyched and confident about my new role as head cook. Now I had the chance to put soulful delectables on each customer's plate. I remembered the cooks of Dipti Nivas and worked as silently as possible. It wasn't always possible, however, since my co-workers were often cracking me up, and I do so love to laugh.

It was challenging work. Our restaurant was far less organized than the one where I was trained. Nothing was prepared, so I had to hustle to chop every ingredient for curries, soups, casseroles, etc. I'd often turn a trip to the walk-in (a large refrigerator) as an opportunity to intensely pray for the capacity to get the job done.

Somehow I got through each day, cooking in the morning and either waitressing or filling orders in the afternoon. It was exhausting, but also rewarding. One time one of the waitresses came up to me with three dollars saying her customer said it was for the cook who made the curry. Was it really the cooking? I would usually imagine light pouring into the food as I would make it. I like to think that was the magic ingredient. As a matter of fact, ever since those days at the restaurant, imagining light inundating my work has been an ongoing pursuit. I think it greatly contributed to my success as a teacher. Years later, when I taught 5th grade, my students continuously said I was the best teacher they ever had. Even their parents agreed. Meditating with them each morning and imagining light pouring into their hearts surely made that success possible.

But success is never guaranteed. I was about to face that reality in a rather startling way. After only a few months as the cook at Jyoti Bihanga, a role that took years of training, preparation and sacrifice was about to abruptly end. I received a phone call one morning from my Centre leader. It was short and to the point. As compassionately as he could, he told me that Guru called him and said I was to no longer work at the restaurant.

A wave of shock washed over me, lessoned ever so slightly by his next comment, "But Guru said you can eat there for free for the rest of your life."

My mind had a hard time grasping Guru's message. I reeled in shock for weeks. I had weathered various scoldings from Guru over the years, but nothing like this one. It didn't make any sense. I could find no reason why my Guru would fire me. I had no vital problems with the boys, which was typically why a disciple gets asked to leave an enterprise. And I wondered why Guru tempered his harsh sentence with the free meals. It was all very perplexing and emotionally devastating.

I was facing the biggest hurdle of my spiritual life. I knew the correct approach was to cheerfully accept the wishes of the Master. He does, after all, have much greater vision than I. But my pride was smashed, and my ego left in the dust. I couldn't even get myself to show my face to the other disciples. Guru's generous offer of free meals for life would go to waste.

Although I knew that a Master's scolding is always to help the disciple make the fastest progress and stay on track, I was incapable of cheerful acceptance, or even angry acceptance. For me, his request was a roundabout way of saying, "I'd like you to leave my path." For it was hard to separate the restaurant from the Centre. It's Guru's restaurant really, just as it is his Centre.

Rationalizing it this way I soon came to the realization that I should leave the path. Since I couldn't even face the San Diego disciples I gave myself one last chance and went back to San Francisco. I thought perhaps I'd feel okay with remaining in that Centre. But even a change of Centres couldn't wipe away the firm belief I had formed that Guru no longer wanted me as his disciple. My mind won that battle.

I shared my plight with just a few disciples: a close friend, Bitapi, and a male co-worker at the San Francisco restaurant from the time when I trained there. At this point I didn't care about obedience anymore. I allowed myself to freely chat with this boy, telling all. He had already been scolded once for talking too much to me months earlier. He reciprocated, telling me of his woes and growing disinterest with remaining on the path. Our shared feelings about leaving, together with a strong sense that we were a good match for each other, led to our decision to leave together. One week after arriving in San Francisco I was driving a packed car with Jigisha and his belongings to start a new life in Santa Barbara.

In a snap, we were gone. The path was behind us, each one carrying the memories of six remarkable and life-illumining years. We had both become disciples in 1980.

We fled, so to speak, to Santa Barbara, California: a place we both loved and hoped to settle in. Neither of us had much money so we set up camp next to a beautiful lake nestled in the mountains. Within two weeks we were married. Luckily, I never cared much for traditional ceremonies. And since all our friends were disciples to whom we surely were considered outcasts, no ceremony was had. We called a retired judge, pulled in an old lady walking down the street as a witness and voila, we were officially a couple, bonded by marriage 'til divorce do us part.

Our campsite became our honeymoon getaway. For three weeks nature was our home. She gave us solace and time to reflect on how to approach life all over again.

I was more fortunate than I could imagine, hooking up with Jigisha. We both had tremendous love for our Guru, the spiritual life and maintaining the spiritual standard we had reached on the path. We quickly created a celibate relationship that would last our whole marriage. Circumstances led to our outer leaving, but our inner connections with our Guru remained strong. I would eventually discover the reason behind that circumstance many years later.

I owe it to Jigisha, his purity and his commitment to spiritual growth, for keeping my spiritual aspirations alive. The meaning of his spiritual name shined even off the path. Jigisha means the seeker with the most intense aspiration to conquer ignorance once and for all.

We talked, we laughed, and we reminisced for hours on end. I was so happy to have male companionship. It created a sense of balance inside me. Making the transition from being on a spiritual path and all that entailed to going at it virtually alone was huge. The sense of community was gone and close friends were no longer available. We helped each other through it, becoming dearest friends in the process. I married someone I hardly knew, but in my heart the sense of surety was solid. I had not even a flicker of doubt that Jigisha was right for me. It was as if our marriage was an experience I was meant to have. I still wonder if Guru set things up as he did to make it happen. I was in heaven, perhaps the happiest I'd ever been. Not having a companion was the hardest thing for me while on the path. Yet the path filled my hunger for the divine. Now my challenge was to keep both alive at the same time.

We must have succeeded in doing that, for six and a half years later the unthinkable happened. It was about 5 am when the phone's ring startled us awake. It was Ashrita, Guru's message deliverer. "Lynn?" he said. (I hadn't been given a spiritual name yet). "This is Ashrita. I'm calling to give you a message from Guru. He said you and Jigisha can come back to the path together if you want."

Jigisha and I were astounded, touched and grateful beyond words. We had grown to miss our experiences on the path and especially meditating with Guru. It gave our lives so much more purpose and intensity. There would be Christmas trips so we could travel the world again with Guru, and countless opportunities to be of service to others in a way that meant the most to us. And there would be a group to regularly meditate with. Without hesitation I responded to Ashrita that we would love to come back.

By this time we had settled in San Diego, since neither of us could find work in Santa Barbara. Jigisha owned and ran a music store and I worked as a college counselor and instructor. I used my time off the path to earn a Master's Degree and to learn Spanish in between our constant adventures throughout the southwest. We easily crammed twenty years of mutual experience into six and a half, spending all our free time together.

Our return to the path would now be as members of the San Diego Centre. My role as the link would continue. My role as a wife and a disciple, however, created new complications. First, I was shocked to discover that guys still flung their flirtatious nets over me. I thought I would avoid that old problem being married. Not hardly. Guys don't seem to care if you're married or not. But even harder to deal with was the attitude my husband had toward me as his wife. It was something that never came up when we were off the path. Now that we were back Jigisha acted as if I was his mistake.

We got along great when we were away from disciples, but amidst them I was treated very differently. Jigisha behaved liked he wanted nothing to do with me, creating an energy that felt extremely alienating. But since it only came up when we were with disciples, we managed to remain happily married for a fairly long time. There were so many activities that we quickly immersed ourselves in that this issue remained unexplosive for the time being. It would eventually surface in full force later on.

For the most part, returning to the path brought many good things. For one, the mystery of being fired from the restaurant was solved. Another disciple was involved after all. It was a girl whom Guru had made manager of Jyoti Bihanga. The problem, however, was that she never informed any of us of that position, at least not until after I had left. Unaware of her rightful authority I had criticized her bossy insistence of how the restaurant should be run to the Centre leader. The next day I was asked to leave. It was after I returned to the path that this disciple divulged this bit of information along with an apology.

Interestingly, I never held it against her or Guru. Perhaps because, in the end, I was quite happy with the way the puzzle pieces of my life came together: held tight with the glue of gratitude.

CHAPTER SIX

ROUNDTWO- BACK ON THE PATH

In fact, the appreciation I felt for being given a second chance at discipleship was overwhelming. It created an intense need to give back. I was consumed with wanting to serve the Supreme by expanding Guru's mission. So I set out on a bold undertaking: single-handedly opening seven Meditation Centres in seven cities. I chose mostly unchartered land – the Southwest: Las Vegas, Tucson, Phoenix, Santa Fe, Los Alamos, Albuquerque, and Salt Lake City.

Ablaze with determination, I felt unstoppable energy. The enthusiasm that brightened my early disciple years rose again in full magnificence. But, unlike my early years, I now had 13 years of meditation behind me. I was in the perfect position to do what I had dreamed of doing since childhood – kindle humanity's inspiration to create a better world, albeit, a tiny slice of humanity. The spiritual roller coaster I stepped onto 13 years ago was taking a fast and exciting turn. Little did I know it was heading upward towards the biggest thrill of my ride.

It felt like the five parts of my being were, for once, in full cooperation. My physical was energized, my vital determined, my mind focused, and my heart and soul were flooding me with peace, power and joy. I'd often spontaneously feel my heart-center as if it was being magically activated. It was the best I could ask for. I had a partner and companion who fully supported what I wanted to do for the path. I didn't have to live the roommate lifestyle with a bunch of girls; something I never cared for. And I could outwardly be with my Guru again. My life was complete. Unfortunately, nothing ever lasts. Knowing this, I often took a moment from whatever I was doing to savor the feeling of real satisfaction. I seemed to intuitively know that my "on fire" state of intense aspiration would eventually peter out.

An incredible sense of confidence filled those years. Undaunted by other peoples' doubt, I plunged forward with my plan. Almost everyone I mentioned it to said I was wasting my time. They insisted there would be no interest in meditation in cities like Las Vegas and Salt Lake City. I knew in my heart they were wrong. And since I needed nothing from those people to continue I worked alone to bring my dream to fruition.

I'd mail out flyers to probable receptive businesses and organizations, contact radio stations with public service announcements, and book community rooms as a place to offer a free "Learn to Meditate" class.

The experience was utterly fulfilling and sometimes a bit humorous; like the time I gave a class in Los Alamos, New Mexico. There I was, a 30-something woman, helping a room full of male mathematicians and physicists to discover something within them they had never been able to find on their own. But the most challenging location was Salt Lake City, not because of the people, but because of me.

I'd often arrive days before a class so I could put up more flyers. But as I walked the streets of Salt Lake City I could hear myself scoffing at the people. I had so much negativity toward the Mormon religion, especially in their practice of advocating having numerous children. I even had a man stop me on the street and ask me where my kids were. Feeling this way bothered me. I felt hypocritical. Here I was advocating acceptance and oneness, yet all I could do was judge. My negativity had to go. I did not want to stand before the people of Salt Lake City in this mind frame. So the day before the first scheduled class I drove to the top of a mountain that overlooked the city. There I sat, praying and meditating to illumine my judgments.

Within an hour I felt unimaginably different. It was as if the city below me had entered into my heart, and in so doing it morphed my negativity into understanding and acceptance. I was literally seeing the city and its people with new eyes. My judgments about a religion that encourages having more kids to build its following were replaced with admiration for a very prayerful people. I was seeing Salt Lake City's strengths rather than her weaknesses. My focus simply shifted. It was clear that this wasn't my imagination when I descended the mountain and drove around the city again. The negativity had vanished.

The next morning I stood before a packed house of sincere spiritual seekers and gave a four-hour workshop. I discovered what I had intuitively known. Throngs of people, most of them raised Mormon were looking for a deeper spiritual connection than their religion could offer. I left that class with the mountaintop under my feet, and soon had a meditation group established.

I had the same experience again in Las Vegas. The meditation classes were filled. As one participant said, "If you can aspire in Las Vegas with the constant onslaught of temptations, you can rest assured that you're making spiritual progress and you'll be able to meditate anywhere." What was clear was that spiritually hungry people live everywhere and religion isn't fulfilling the hunger.

CHAPTER SEVEN
THE PEACE RUN

After spending two years opening meditation Centres in seven cities I was presented with an even bigger challenge. The longing of humanity for inner peace and a world imbued with peace was made strikingly evident during the greatest event I ever undertook: the Peace Run.

The Peace Run was a 50-state, 11,000-mile relay run, complete with a flaming torch and an international team of runners. About 12 of us took turns running seven to ten miles a day. We visited schools, retirement homes and government officials along the way with one message: for peace to happen in the world it has to happen within each individual first. Our talks inspired young people to value its pursuit and to make an effort towards bringing peace forward in their own lives.

As we ran into their auditoriums kids greeted us like we were a group of famous rock stars. For four months we were heroes in the eyes of so many people.

Participating in the Peace Run was an especially gratifying experience. Everything I loved was wrapped into one perfect package: the vastness of nature, inspiring others, running across spectacular countryside and embracing the whole of our country. It felt as if my whole life was one long preparation for that single event. The experiences gleaned from it were as vast as the country we crossed. We not only had to deal with the fatigue of running and barely sleeping in a different place every night, but also with each other. The best and the worst come out of people in these kinds of situations. We sometimes wondered how we were going to spread the message of peace when we would sometimes miserably fail at spreading it amongst ourselves.

Events would often unfold in a way that made me feel I was being monitored by an unseen force. Every thought and every action seemed to have an immediate reaction; like the time I ran to the beat of Bob Dylan. I was having a ball silently singing along to one Dylan tune after another. I usually listened to meditative music, but on that day I felt like rocking out on the run. Within half an hour a car rolled up next to me, and a very angry man yelled out, "Do you really think you're making a difference!" Then he sped off. His tone was so venomous that my whole body began shaking. Like a slap in the face, the message I got was clear: if I am going to spread the message of peace during the Peace Run I have to be focused on peace while I'm running.

I vowed to never listen to rock music again while running. Moreover, this experience showed me why Sri Chinmoy advised his students not to listen to rock music. There is simply no comparison to the heights of consciousness a seeker can reach without rock music. However high we think it can take us, or however inspiring we think the lyrics are, it is nowhere near the height and depth of inner silence.

The very next day, with headphones packed away, I made a sincere effort to have my thoughts be on peace and light inundating the earth. And again a car slowly rolled up to me. A very robust, African-American woman rolled down her window and emptied her wallet into my hand. As her eyes teared up she called out to me, "I'm in no shape to run with you, but I want to support what you all are doing for our planet. So please take what I have and God bless you girl!"

Make of this what you will, but for me it couldn't be clearer. Thoughts matter, and they matter far more than we realize. Needless to say, the intensity with which I stayed focused on all things divine just turned up several notches.

Taking the time off to do the Peace Run nearly cost me my home. It was a sacrifice of job, money, and comfort. But the inner wealth I received was unparalleled. We were planting seeds of peace in the minds and hearts of thousands.

I had inklings of being an instrument of the Supreme before, but nothing as profound as what the Peace Run offered. Sometimes, tired and weary after a sleepless night due to a teammate's snoring, I'd find myself flying down the road. My legs moved as if a swift and agile runner had taken over my body, leaving me to bask in the glorious scenery. At night I'd often put my experiences to poetry:

From the depths of my soul
A battle cry resounds.
It rises like fierce winds
Determined and sure
Hurling thoughts to horizon's abyss.
Energy in every color and form
Percolates around me
As nature's glory penetrates my core.
My breath dances on waves of joy.
I breathe, I run, I soar.

And what an awesome sensation it was to soar so effortlessly over high mountain passes, like the time I ran over the Colorado Rockies. So many people honked their horns in support and admiration, cheering me along as they whizzed by. Anyone could see that running that pass was no joke, and yet it felt downhill. It was like the physical had merged with the spiritual, allowing its Light to take over. How I wish I could forever maintain that state, but I'm clearly not at that level yet.

My first Peace Run experience was an exceptional one in that way. Over the next six years I repeated it three more times, each one successively shorter than the preceding one: three months, then two months and finally only one month. But none of the successive runs were as physically effortless as the first. As a matter of fact, by the last Peace Run I had to push one foot in front of the other to cover a distance that seemed endless. My state of consciousness had everything to do with the difficulty. I just wasn't aspiring as intensely as I remember in the first 1995 event. So yet again I was reminded of the incredible power thought has when it is focused on Light, and what it can enable our bodies to do.

The Peace Run was also the perfect venue to put my Guru's teachings to practice, like making one's state of consciousness a priority. Over the years Guru passed on many of these tidbits of truth. Another one of my favorites that I practice everyday in my work as a teacher is to never squelch enthusiasm for any reason. To compromise enthusiasm for greater efficiency, for example, would do more harm than good. I now value enthusiasm and view it as something precious, in the same way I value being in a good consciousness. I had to make this choice with a teammate one day while we were driving to our evening campsite.

An Unconventional Pursuit

My team of three girls had just finished running our miles and I was the navigator. But our driver was insistent that she knew the way. I noticed her anger began to rise each time I suggested an alternate route. Since I had the map it was clear to me that she was mistaken. So I asked myself, "Do I continue to convince her of her mistake, knowing full well it will result in tremendous negativity, or do I knowingly let us go in the wrong direction so as to maintain the harmony, letting her realize her mistake in time." We were all enjoying each other's company so much on that drive that it seemed silly to sacrifice it just to save time. So we drove on and on and on, until finally my dear friend and teammate realized her folly. It was wonderful to watch. Not because I wanted her to see that she was wrong, but because I saw how happy we all remained despite the huge detour. The girl in the back seat was asleep at the time of our discussion so she never knew that I had allowed us to go in the wrong direction. And my driving teammate very apologetically admitted her mistake as we backtracked a very long expanse of highway. We all laughed our way back to the campsite and arrived a good three hours late. For me, it was a well earned three hours. Happiness really is priceless. And, needless to say, I always offered to drive whenever that girl was on my team.

Running through all the states has to be one of the highlights of my life. The only other experience that stands out as powerfully was the moment I received my spiritual name. Each state had a distinct quality that was almost tangibly felt, as we'd cross one border to another. It was uncanny, too, how even the topography and flora would often change with each state.

The most dramatic change, however, was passing through the northern states after leaving Washington. All traces of other cultures vanished. We asked ourselves where were the African-Americans, Hispanics, Asians, Middle-easterners, and on and on. It became one long route of white Anglo-Americans broken by only a few isolated American-Indian communities. And it remained that way until we reached Chicago.

Having lived my life in the diverse state of California, entering Chicago was surprisingly refreshing. After so many weeks of forests, rolling wheat grass and farmland, I thought the bustle of a metropolis would be shocking. Instead, being surrounded by a multitude of cultures was invigorating. Each one had its own unique way of expressing their desire for peace. All the tiny drops of individuality merged into one river of hope.

When the Peace Run finally ended on August 15th at the United Nations my whole being melted into tears of gratitude. Our team of 12 runners stood on a stage amidst roaring rounds of applause. And the ear-to-ear smile of my Guru revealed how proud he was of us. Then all the other teams that completed Peace Runs across Europe and among 70 other countries joined us on stage. We had all made incredible efforts to kindle peace throughout the world. Being a participant to that end was the greatest accomplishment, and the most fulfilling form of service I have ever done.

I often wonder how I will ever surpass that achievement. Then I remind myself that every student I ever inspired to improve is a great accomplishment, and that we all can continuously be of service to the Supreme in humanity in as many ways as there are people.

The American Peace Run Team at the United Nations.

PEACE RUN

*No greater freedom found
Then an arm stretched to the skies
With a flame dancing God's reflection
In my eyes.*

*Aspiration hidden awakens without effort
With body, vital and mind
Synchronized to the rhythm
Of the ever upward climb.*

*Grace breathes in
Gratitude breathes out
As footfalls, like oars,
Push toward peace sublime.*

- Kinkani

CHAPTER EIGHT
MY SPIRITUAL NAME

The one experience that was as fulfilling as the Peace Run, though much shorter in time, was the moment I received my spiritual name. I waited 13 years for that sacred moment, largely due to having left the path for six and a half years. Most of Guru's disciples receive their spiritual names in person. Guru meditates on the individual while placing a paper with their name on it on their head. I often wondered what that would feel like. I never will be able to say; Guru gave my name to another disciple to deliver to me in San Diego. It was a blessing in disguise.

When I first heard that someone was bringing my name to me from New York I had mixed feelings. I was elated that I finally got a name and disappointed that I didn't get that rare, one-on-one moment with my Guru. Guru asked that we meditate before reading our name. I meditated for half an hour, clutching the envelope to my heart. I thought it was about to burst out of its chakra by the time I opened the envelope. I knew then, as I carefully unsealed the fold, that it was highly unlikely that I would ever have reached such a deep state of meditation in front of Guru with a thousand people looking on.

Guru gave me the chance to have the most significant inner experience possible, and it certainly was. As I pulled out the heart-shaped paper adorned with Guru's bird drawings, I could barely make out the letters of my name through the flood of tears. It was as if Guru was right there blessing me on the head. And with no interference of my mind, ego or fear my heart could blossom in its full effulgence. I wiped away the tears to find the letter K. Then slowly the rest of the name came into focus...Kinkani. I immediately loved the sound of it. I read on: "The sweet-small heart-bell constantly ringing to love and serve the Supreme always in His own way."

I sat there pressing my name to my heart for another two hours in utter bliss. My name is the most significant thing I have been given. Guru said the name he gives a disciple describes his or her most predominant inner qualities and that we could realize God just by chanting it regularly; yet, he says, no one does.

I decided to chant it while I was meditating in Guru's presence one day while we were in Hawaii. I was seated just a few feet from Guru with a small group of people. As I chanted I could barely believe my ears. I actually heard the sound of a bell ringing in my heart. It was so real it almost shocked me out of my meditation. Luckily, its beautiful, delicate sound pulled me in closer and filled me with unbelievable joy. "That's me, Kinkani! The little bell!" I exclaimed to myself. Unfortunately, I've never heard it again.

Interestingly, as a little girl, my mother used to call me Tintina. She said she liked to call me that because it had a ring to it. She must have intuitively known.

We probably all intuitively know what our predominant spiritual qualities are. Many years before receiving my name I wrote what I thought they were in my journal. It read: "Love, service and sweetness." The ringing bell part totally eluded me.

CHAPTER NINE
PRAYERS ANSWERED

Being a disciple of a spiritual Master has many benefits, but one is alarmingly so: the tendency for prayers to be answered. Some of my disciple friends would not agree with this, but for me it is clear. Having a God-realized Guru of a very high caliber is like a personal Federal Express to the Supreme. My prayers over the years have often resulted in immediate response. I made one of these prayers when I was working as a college counselor. After eight years of that position I started to yearn for something more directly related to Sri Chinmoy's path.

I had a cushy job; one that paid well for little hours and was reasonably interesting. But I was completely willing to give it up for something more spiritually fulfilling. I'd often find myself praying in my cushy office for that opportunity to happen. Then, one day, Guru asked my husband and I to move to San Francisco and open a divine enterprise: a health food store.

Being asked was an honor, as it is an uncommon event. And since I was dying to do something more connected to the path, it was perfect, but certainly not easy. We had bought a beautiful home in the San Diego area and would have to sell it to afford opening a business. I cringe at what that house would be worth now.

And yet it was well worth it. Working in our health food store, which Guru named: The Strength-Length of a New Life, was the best job I ever had. I was in heaven. I read health and nutrition books every night in an effort to be at least somewhat competent.

At first, I felt a bit insecure about the whole venture. It was a field I knew nothing about. But I did have faith in my Guru and I knew he would never ask us to do anything we didn't have the capacity for. Sure enough, I not only developed a real passion for heath and nutrition, but I excelled at it too. Customers loved coming in our store, especially workers from a nearby new-age bookstore. It was a joy to help people find natural forms of healing and to find my hours of research pay off with countless success stories. In the end, the store paved the way for a whole new career.

We had created a kind of temple amidst the restless chaos of the city. Inside the store colors of blue, gold and white softly framed shelves of healing magic, fragrant soaps, incense and packaged foods. Soulful music winged the air as customers were transported to a higher consciousness as soon as they stepped through the door.

While most health food stores are earthy, ours was definitely heavenly, and people loved it. Many customers said they just liked standing in the store and soaking in the peace. That was a great compliment, though it would have been nice if they spent a little more money while standing there.

After three years we had to liquidate the store and go out of business. It just wasn't profitable. Although I loved working there, it had been three long years of pretty uncomfortable living arrangements. My husband, a musician, was completely out of his element, unless a guitar-playing customer walked in. Then it became a spontaneous jam session.

Since we had no money to rent a place for ourselves, Jigisha rigged a shower in the back of the store and made the coat closet his bedroom. I slept on the floor in the corner of another disciple's room. Three years of that was about all I could take, so from that standpoint closing the store was a relief. Luckily I found immediate employment as a teacher at a private elementary school. Jigisha moved to New York. My marriage to Jigisha entered rough waters from the very start of the business. We had different opinions about almost everything. But even as that worked itself out our relationship grew increasingly distant. Whatever oneness we had achieved until then broke into "twoness". It was no longer a happy and fulfilling relationship. It wasn't even a friendship. I gave it another full year after closing the store, but to no avail, I asked for a divorce.

I was on fire with aspiration and determination when I came back to the path. But I could feel the weight of unsettled emotions slowly snuff out my enthusiasm to remain on the path. I was back to where I was when I first joined the path: single and living with a group of girls – a combination that has never sat well with me. To at least eliminate the bad taste of the latter I emptied all my earnings into a studio apartment. I barely scraped by. The dot com craze had escalated rental costs to astronomical levels. And though I reveled in the peace and privacy of my own space, I struggled with not having a partner. I simply do better with a partner. For me, it's like adding water to a parched plant. I flourish and thrive, so long as the relationship goes well.

Jigisha and I had lived like brother and sister for practically our entire 16-year marriage. I wasn't after sex. I wanted a companion to share life with. Acknowledging this to myself meant I had to leave Sri Chinmoy's path again.

I respect Guru's standards on the path. Every standard he has asked of his disciples has made perfect sense to me. Guru's path is for the sincere spiritual seekers who want a life outside the ordinary. And in so doing, reap the inner fruits of the extraordinary. I have witnessed over and over, how easily our spiritual focus is shifted by even the slightest interference. You notice someone eyeing you and in a snap your thoughts change course, and if it goes on long enough your life changes course too. Or a tragedy happens and in a snap your love for the divine becomes rage. You inherit a fortune and in a snap you are all consumed by wealth. So to not allow the romantic mixing of disciples on the path is understandable.

What is clear to me, after 23 years on the path, is that Sri Chinmoy gives his all to help his disciples to be happy. We are given chance after chance to bring our best forward, and endless opportunities to blossom into self-giving instruments of the Supreme.

Guru must have infinite patience to wait while we flounder in our ignorance. Yet, some ruthlessly criticize him when their petty desires are left unsatisfied. These people remind me of children who cry when they don't get what they want.

Without a doubt, my Master's role was clear. He showed me how to make myself as receptive as possible to divine Light, and how to approach the Supreme to make communing with divinity possible. He also taught me how to bring purity, peace, dynamism and other divine qualities into my body, vital, mind and heart. But most important of all, my Master taught me how to keep the flame of spiritual aspiration burning bright. For in the end, it is our aspiration that will eventually rise up to meet God's descending grace.

Most of us simply cannot fathom a Master's ways. But let us not condemn what we do not understand with our limited minds and flailing egos. Every spiritual Master, from Krishna to Buddha to Christ and all others, has been misunderstood. Perhaps it is time that humanity, for once, embrace the Masters, past and present, and learn from the rare opportunity we are given to see true goodness spreading its Light.

How many will know
The magic of the Master's touch
How in silence sublime
He carries us

By what deed did grace descend
And why do my eyes
Even as they fill with light
So easily shift toward night

- Kinkani

Many other prayers have been answered over the years, but so too have written requests. Some of them dealt with physical problems like runner's knee, and a herniated disc, to name a few. After suffering from those injuries for months Guru would take them away after reading my letters. His compassion and concern were unlimited. And he expressed them in ways that often surprised me, like the time he invited me to his house to celebrate my birthday.

I knew exactly what the customers of my health food store meant when they said they just liked standing in the store. That was how I felt inside Guru's house. The first time I was invited to witness the Master's abode for an extended length of time, not just passing through, was on my birthday. I had made a special trip to New York to be in my Master's presence. Most mornings it was possible to meditate with him at Aspiration Ground, the open-air court where most of the functions take place during celebrations. Some local disciples would show up there for a few minutes each morning before going to work. The many opportunities to meditate with Guru are another very special component of his path. Sri Chinmoy's Guru, Sri Aurobindo, was only available in person once a year. We were, indeed, lucky.

I was meditating in Aspiration Ground on the morning of my birthday, when I received the message that I was invited to Guru's house that night. I could barely believe it. I had been a disciple for 15 years, but this was the first time Guru would honor my birthday with a special meditation at his house. The only way to describe how I felt is to imagine a big lump of melting gratitude; nothing else existed at that moment.

From start to finish, the whole experience was like a fairy tale, written to perfection. First, I was chauffeured to Guru's house by another disciple, who went around and picked up other special invitees. Walking toward the front door felt much like being in line for prasad, focusing on my heart and praying for receptivity. If ever there was a time when I wanted my mind to cooperate it was then.

Inside the house Guru sat in a stuffed chair with the boys seated to his left and the girls to his right. It is laid out in such a way that the girls and boys cannot see each other at all. And we only see the back or side of Guru's head.

Since Guru isn't looking at anyone there is no vying for his attention – a pleasant reprise.

I found an open patch of carpet near a wall and propped myself into position. Getting into a meditative state was amazingly easy. Just breathing the air was like swimming in ambrosia. "So this is what it's like at Guru's house," I thought. I felt truly blessed. If there was ever a Shangri-la this was it.

For a while, a video played with some kind of comedy. I wasn't paying much attention to it. All I wanted to do was meditate. Then, suddenly, Guru called for a disciple boy to stand in front of him. It was his birthday too. The house fell silent as we all drank in the Light that seemed to pour from the air. Then it was my turn. Unfortunately, when Guru called my name my heart sank to my feet, cut loose, no doubt, by the thunderous shaking. I wished I had a Valium. I definitely had a better meditation when Guru wasn't meditating right on me. Yet I could still feel his Light pour into me. It seemed like such a long time, though it was probably only a few minutes.

Since then, I was invited for several more birthdays to meditate with Guru at his house. I will cherish those moments to the end of my life.

Meditating with Guru in his home on my birthday.

CHAPTER TEN
OFF AGAIN

A whirlwind of thoughts swirled inside my head as I clutched the phone. Within, a battle was raging with the soldiers of swift progress mercilessly fighting off squadrons of desires. Do I stay or do I leave? As commander of my battleground I had to make a decision. I could no longer uphold the standards of the path I had chosen 23 years ago.

Then, as quickly as the phone call ended, the battle ceased, and my future changed course. With the message delivered that I had chosen to leave Guru's path, I could stop battling with my discontent and start building a new life.

I am, nevertheless, amazed at the power of our human nature to override our divine nature. Even after 23 years of higher experiences I was still willing to sacrifice being surrounded by divinity for human companionship. Is it any wonder human evolution is so slow?

The hardest part of leaving Sri Chinmoy's path the second time was being completely alone. Finding new friends and a partner in a society of primarily outer-oriented people isn't easy. Luckily, at least, my work as a 5th grade teacher gave me an opportunity to pass on some of the wisdom gleaned from years of spiritual discipline. It helped, too, that I was spiritually fed by spiritually giving. The relationship with my students was like having 20 kids. So long as I can inspire others to reach for a higher consciousness my life has meaning. Undoubtedly, this was my Guru's most significant lesson, and the answer to the fulfillment that I was looking for as a teenager.

In the end, four classes of elementary school kids got an education they'll never forget. We meditated every morning, learned to value the power of thoughts and practiced character building in every lesson. I saw students transform before my eyes, and parents bow in gratitude for fostering that transformation. One mother even said, "Thank you for giving me my daughter back." Her daughter had almost completely fallen into a self-destructive, arrogant, hateful and hurtful way of being, and was nearly expelled from school. In my class, perhaps for the first time in her life, she saw and grew into her own inner beauty and Light. That girl is not only the pride of her mother; she is the pride of my career.

But showing young people the beauty of their own Light is one thing, finding an adult with a child's eagerness to learn about it is another. So in my quest for a partner I took the help of technology and tried my luck with computer dating.

There are some real benefits to becoming sensitive to people's consciousness. It served me well while using the Craig's List web site. Each plea for a date revealed far more than the words themselves. It became an amusing challenge to tune into the person's consciousness hidden within the words. I tried some of those spiritual dating sites too, but the new age grooviness was an immediate turn off. I don't want to date a man who calls himself "Starchaser". I thought that surely there had to be men out there who led normal, balanced lives but who also had spiritual aspiration. What I found was that most men who stated that they were spiritually oriented also were pretty arrogant about it. Having a spiritual discussion with someone who thinks of himself as above everybody is not inspiring. I quickly added humility to my quest.

After six misses, although all were pretty decent, I finally stumbled on a potential winner. That thing behind the words, call it a vibration, was incredibly compelling for one man, Dean. My heart was practically yelling at me to pursue Dean further, but my mind could only find a list of objections. He was too short. He had a kid. He had a passion for sports I didn't do and it went on and on. But despite what he said, what I felt from his writing was undeniable. I had to respond.

It turns out my heart was right. Dean was that perfect blend of humility, spiritual aspiration and mental/emotional balance that I was looking for. Proving to me, once again, that the inner world is the most important.

Had I not made that initial leap into the spiritual life at age 20 and practiced its disciplines for most of my adult life, it is unlikely I would have cultivated the array of inner skills necessary to achieve what I have. And I certainly would not have had the depth of inner experiences.

What I am faced with now is the daunting task of spiritually moving forward without the help of a spiritual path. There is no denying that a path accelerates one's progress. It is like learning a foreign language at an immersion school, rather than in a classroom in the States. The language, without even an utterance of English at home or at school, surrounds you. Likewise, on a spiritual path, especially one with a living Master, a seeker is inundated with Light and surrounded by others who are aspiring for the same goal.

My tired body that would rather relax in front of the TV today, in the past, would have been learning new songs, working on some project or any number of things. I would be transcending my capacities and immersed in a soulful consciousness on a constant basis.

There was always the sense of being pushed forward while on the path. But off it, it has become my responsibility to push myself. It's like being on a slow jog compared to the high-speed sprint of my early years. It seems my ride on the rapids has reached placid waters. I've had to get out the oars and paddle.

At this rate, it may take eons to reach my goal, but I am not alone. For I have gained a deep and solid connection with my Guru that defies space and time. His guidance, his consciousness, and his love reside in my heart more powerfully than I could ever have imagined. I need only stay focused there.

Overall, being a student of a spiritual Master revealed an inner world of Light and delight, and an outer life of constant transformation. I am hard-pressed to find anything that comes close to the heights and depths of consciousness that abound on his path. To have a Master of Sri Chinmoy's caliber is an unparalleled experience whatever the length of time. A seeker need only be receptive.

To all those who are looking for a spiritual teacher, just know: when we find our teacher we will have found the most precious gift possible on earth. It is then up to us whether or not we cherish that gift. If we do, sooner than we think, we may find ourselves in the Lap of the Supreme.

WANTING

Sometimes I just want to pour my heart out to the cosmos.
For every drop of love
To touch every breath of God's creation.

To see my love touch a star
And make it burn brighter.
To smile and smile and know that by it
The whole world breathes lighter.

To feel my gratitude flow
Like a river of light
Into the endless sky of blue,
Rivaling even nature's own breathtaking hues.
And finally, Lord, to return to You.

And God's eye will shine in every human eye.
And God's love becomes the heartbeat of mankind.

- Kinkani

ABOUT THE AUTHOR

Kinkani Mursinna became a disciple of the spiritual Master, Sri Chinmoy, in 1980 at the age of 20. After 23 years she outwardly left his spiritual path, no longer participating in disciple activities. Yet, inwardly, the guidance of her Guru and the presence of his consciousness live on. Since his passing on October 11, 2007 his guidance has become even more profound.

Kinkani lives with her husband near San Francisco, California where she continues to meditate regularly and practice the disciplines her Guru encouraged. Although no longer running marathons, she continues an active lifestyle of running, biking and hiking. She keeps the experience of physical self-transcendence alive by pursuing the art of surfing northern California's frigid coastline and by backpacking into the high elevations of California's mountains.

Her career life has been in counseling and education where she used her Master's of Science degree in Educational Counseling to teach young and old from pre-school through college. She also conducts presentations for students intended to increase their awareness of the power of thoughts and to offer them simple meditation exercises to experience inner peace.

ABOUT SRI CHINMOY

Sri Chinmoy is a renowned spiritual leader, peace luminary and friend of humanity. Born in East Bengal, India in 1931, he was the youngest of seven children. From the age of twelve, he lived in a spiritual community in southern India where he was a champion sprinter and decathlete. His life of intense spiritual practice included meditating for up to 14 hours a day, together with writing poetry, essays and devotional songs, doing selfless service and practicing athletics. While still in his early teens, he had many profound inner experiences and attained spiritual realization. He remained in the ashram for 20 years.

Following an inner command, Sri Chinmoy came to America in 1964, living in New York City until his passing in 2007. There he led the Peace Meditation at the United Nations for 37 years with delegates and staff at the invitation of Secretary General U Thant. Through myriad creative public offerings — including Peace Concerts, the Peace Run, and the Sri Chinmoy Peace Blossoms family — Sri Chinmoy traveled the globe to offer the message that each of us has boundless treasures within.

Sri Chinmoy lead an active life, demonstrating most vividly that spirituality is not an escape from the world, but a means of transforming it. He has written hundreds of books, which include plays, poems, stories, essays, commentaries and answers to questions on spirituality. He has painted thousands of widely exhibited mystical paintings and composed thousands of devotional songs.

Sri Chinmoy's achievements as a weight lifter have also earned him considerable renown. To demonstrate that inner peace gained through meditation can be a tangible source of outer strength, he has honored more than 2,000 individuals by physically lifting them overhead on a specially constructed platform in an awards program entitled "Lifting Up the World with a Oneness-Heart."

My ultimate goal is for the power of love
To replace the love of power
Within each individual.
My ultimate goal is for the whole world
To walk together in peace and oneness.

- Sri Chinmoy

For further information about Sri Chinmoy's books and distributors:
www.srichinmoybooks.com

For information on how to obtain a copy of this book, or to write a comment:
www.facebook.com/anunconventionalpursuit

An Unconventional Pursuit is also available as an eBook with Amazon and Apple.